Little Fecker!

The Rise of Noel Kelly

NOEL KELLY

Noel Kelly

Copyright © 2014 Noel Kelly
All rights reserved.

ISBN-13: 978-149438?730

LITTLE FECKER!

DEDICATION

I have been fortunate to meet, work and socialise with many great people. You have supported me, through good years and bad. I credit you with my happiness and survival. You are so important.

As this is the first half of a two-part autobiography, I won't go into detail about the significant help I've received. I'll do that in my second book.

Here, for now, I send my deepest heartfelt thanks to my friends and family. You know me well enough to know how much you mean to me.

This book is first and foremost for those closest to my heart: my wife Joan, my sons Sean and Jimmy, my daughters Nicky and Patricia. Thanks for supporting the *Little Fecker*, even now I'm a big old fecker!

I love you all.

Little Fecker in the middle!

NOEL KELLY

Some of the photographs reproduced in this book were taken by the talented staff of the *Coventry Evening Telegraph,* the *Nuneaton Evening Tribune* and the *Nuneaton and Bedworth Trader.* Thank you.

CONTENTS

Ireland: Growing Up Fast...7

To England: Becoming a Man 54

Stepping Up 111

Infatuation: Nuneaton Borough Football Club......126

Fun Times at Manor Park 169

The Most Famous Men in the World 198

Half Time: Analysis...208

Personal Postscript 209

NOEL KELLY

LITTLE FECKER!

Ireland: Growing Up Fast

Granny, Daddy and Jimmy

My earliest memory is my Granny passing away. I was four. She died sitting up in bed, and I was in the room at the time. I ran to Mammy and told her Granny was making funny noises. Someone jumped on a bike to go and find Daddy, but Granny had died before Daddy got back to the house.

We were poor, but some of Granny's family was well off, and they insisted she was buried in the dark. Yes, my Gran was buried at night because the posh ones didn't want their friends to see our poor old house. I'm sure it wasn't Granny's wish.

Granny's death was to change my life forever. I didn't know at the time, but Granny was the only reason that Daddy had stayed with us in Ireland, rather than joining the exodus to England. Granny had begged him to stay with Mammy and their ten children, and told him he would rue the day if he ever went. Perhaps if he had got home before she died, and spoken to her just one more time, she could have told him again how he should stay with us.

But just a week after Granny's funeral, the signal of the steam horn of the Princess Maud screamed goodbye, as Daddy left the Kelly family, on a boat crammed with hundreds of Irish fathers and sons.

The hundreds grew into thousands in the months ahead. It was 1941; Irish labour was desperately needed in England to work in the foundries, down the mines, and to build roads. Maybe Daddy would have had to go even if Granny hadn't died.

Mammy was very attractive and her ten children all loved her dearly. She was a marvellous woman. Her six boys and four girls – Maureen, Benny, Vincie, Rita, Rose, Doney, Me, Bernie, Pat and James – were all born between 1928 and 1939.

We lived in a three-bedroomed single storey cottage on a little back lane crossroads in Kilbride. Mammy and Daddy had little Pat and James in with them, then the four older boys shared one bedroom, the four girls the other.

Aunt Rosie, Maureen, Rita, Mammy, James, Vincie, Benny
Doney, Noel, Bernie, Pat, Rose

LITTLE FECKER!

Daddy left Mammy to fend for herself and us. It was tough – we didn't have social services to care for us, so the order of the day was work or starve. We had one big table and we would all sit down at the same time. Except for Mammy, she hardly ever sat down. There might be fights over the table, especially if Mammy put too much food on one plate. Then it would start, "Why has he got more than me?" Poor Mammy, she was a saint dressed as a skivvy. One way or another she made sure we had two meals, sandwiches for work or school, milk by the gallon and butter by the stone.

We had a big garden, in the season it was full of spuds and the best veg in the country. If there was any money to be had, Saturday was shopping day in Dublin. A supermarket trolley was of little use; a lift on any passing van or pick-up truck was more like it. The hot weather was a curse; sometimes we had to drink the butter.

We had no inside toilet, which was awkward. If you needed to pee in the night, you had to work out which bed the "po" was under. With ten kids sharing two bedrooms, this was an achievement in itself. The only way you knew if there was room in the po was whether your thumb got warm or not. If it was full you had to take it outside and empty it - the big old thing weighed a ton when full, so there was a knack – if it was nearly full it was easier to pee outside than have to carry the night's "collection". Getting caught avoiding po duty was punished by all – if Rita caught me it was: "Ned, you little fecker, have you been outside to pee again?" Of course this woke everyone, and I'd get the job of emptying the po every morning for a week!

And heartache was never very far away. The local farmer and the Garda turned up one day and told Mammy that our three dogs had been worrying his sheep and killing his lambs. I knew it was a lie because the dogs were always tied up during lambing. The farmer insisted he'd seen a trace of blood on one of the dogs. There was no opportunity to fight our corner - the Garda took all three dogs away, and we never saw them again - we were devastated. My first experience of rough justice. Mammy's tears stuck with me.

The war was on, Daddy landed up in the Sterling Metals near Nuneaton. Foundry work – you couldn't find tougher conditions anywhere in the world (as I was later to discover for myself). His gang was turning out 300 incendiary bomb casings every night.

An uncle of ours was killed in an explosion in the foundry – he tried to prevent a pot from exploding by removing it from its housing, but was burned to death when the molten metal blew up in his face.

Back in Ireland, Mammy was left with ten young children, almost all at school age. We shared the responsibilities; manners, discipline, schooling, clothing... shoes! Very often we had none, cardboard from a shoebox and sticky tape to hold them together was a luxury, the state promised on many occasions to shoe us all but they never did.

LITTLE FECKER!

With Daddy now in England, working all these shifts, Mammy assured us it wouldn't be long before the money would start to roll in. On Saturday mornings she would give two of us, usually me and Doney, a list of meat and groceries, and we had to cycle five miles to Ratoath. The money from Daddy was due to be wired to the post office at 10.30, so in excitement we would get there at 9.30 and wait. We sat, in innocent anticipation, and watched the kind lady pushing and pulling the wireless plugs in and out of the old switchboard, desperately hoping that the next one pushed in would be Daddy's money. 11.30 would come and we would still be as hopeful as we'd been two hours earlier – Daddy wouldn't let us down!

12.00 was closing time - the deadline. It came and went. Doney and I could only stare at one another - there were no words to come out. Fighting back tears we'd say something stupid to the lady, like, "Oh, we forgot, Daddy's sending money *next* week!" The lady would look at us so sadly – sometimes she would cry.

All we wanted, all we expected, was a fiver. The thought would hit us: how can we face Mammy without any food, nothing? She knew before we got into the house, of course - riding our bikes instead of wheeling them, empty shopping bags on empty handlebars, blank expressions on our faces. Mammy would go into the bedroom and cry for a long time, not for herself I think, but sad for the man she had loved so much. I'm sure Granny's words would echo in her head, along with the worry of how she would feed her children.

I didn't really understand the situation back then, I guess I thought Mammy might have been worried that Daddy was ill or even dead, but as I've grown up I can only imagine the tortures Mammy must have endured, imagining what distractions could have stopped Daddy from sending money to feed his children.

Mammy went through hell almost every week, but it taught me to never feel sorry for myself. Instead, I did something about it. I rode the five miles to Ratoath one Saturday with a pal. His mother was German, but neither he nor I knew that my Daddy was making bombs to drop on his grandparents' house in Germany. We sat on the wall outside the post office, and I popped in and out every ten minutes to check whether Daddy's money had turned up.

Three big lads sat on the wall opposite, sniggering at us. When I came out of the post office empty handed, they shouted "Waiting for your old feller's telegram?" The shout became a chant, "You'll get no fecking money, your old feller has drunk the fecking lot!"

It was a fair scrap; I wasn't a bad little fighter and I was fuelled by the prospect of no money and another humiliation. I dived on one of the lads and hit him three times; he pushed me away and ran off, crying for his Mammy. The other two ran, and as we chased them they reached a pile of stones, and started throwing. We ducked back behind the wall opposite the post office, and a man chased them away – victory!

We hopped over the wall and ran into the post office, laughing with excitement and relief. The lady behind the counter was smiling, which was very nice to see – this could only mean one thing! And yes, there was a tenner from Daddy! A tenner!

I've smiled a lot in my life, but you will never see a bigger smile on my face as was there as we came out of the post office. The smile didn't fade that much when we noticed that the bastards had come back and jumped on our bicycle wheels, and bust the spokes. I just thought "never mind, we can push them, and we have a tenner!" We could never have ridden the bikes anyway, there was so much grub hanging on the handlebars – we bought everything on Mammy's list and a few treats too!

In the war days, Daddy only came home at Christmas. We all met him off the bus at Rooks Cross and walked the half a mile back to the house. Daddy was pleased to see us but had a strange expression on his face. After a hundred yards or so Daddy just stopped without any reason – we all stopped and looked at him.

His frown changed to a look of serenity, as he let out the longest, loudest fart I ever heard in my life. A big man, he was a gentleman, and he had obviously hung onto whatever was inside him on the whole bus trip from Dublin.

We set off again - of course we kids weren't allowed to disrespect Daddy, so we were all giving each other the eye, hands over our mouths stifling the giggles.

Daddy was laughing inside too – his broad shoulders were shaking for quite a while down the road.

We were so excited to see him, but we were young, and equally excited by what might be in his carriers. Lovely food! Lovely Christmas presents? We would fight to help him carry the brown paper bags.

"No peeking!" he would say in his lovely deep voice, and a smile would light his face. Then we knew there were presents.

When we got to the house, Mammy greeted him with smiles and tears that showed me more than anything what love was. They would stand in the bedroom for what seemed like hours, holding one another very tightly, swaying ever so slightly like they were dancing, hardly a word spoken, just loving one another. Mammy loved Daddy so much, but the happiness was tinged with tension for all of us. We were full of anticipation, hoping that this time Daddy would stay, and not go back to England.

We were hungry, and wondering what was in the bags, but Daddy had taken them into the bedroom. We would have to wait until Christmas Day for the presents. We were awake early. After serving up porridge, Mammy went to the wardrobe and said, "Get in a line". We formed a queue behind her, no particular order but it was important not to be at the back in case the presents ran out. There would be a bit of a scuffle, but Mammy wouldn't start dishing out presents until we had settled, so we did quite quickly.

LITTLE FECKER!

Mammy would stand with her back to us, looking into the bags in the wardrobe, but she wouldn't know who was next in the queue. She would just pick something out of the wardrobe and pass it over her shoulder. There was no wrapping paper, no name tag. It paid you to take the thing, whatever it was - knowing Daddy, he might have bought short and the last one in the queue would get no present, except for a cuddle off Mammy.

This particular Christmas I got a lovely storybook, all coloured pictures. Excited, I sat down and stared at the fantastic front cover. Just as I went to open it, the book disappeared. My sister Rita had grabbed it. She dropped a little cuddly white rabbit in my lap and said, "I'm older than you. You can have the rabbit". Justice, Kelly style.

Just a day or two later, the enjoyment, the excitement, were shattered. Mammy crying in the bedroom, begging Daddy to come home for good. He kissed us all in turn at the bus stop. We waved him goodbye with tears in our eyes and on our cheeks. Mammy cried for days. Our dog Tiny cried and howled along with Mammy. Another year before we would see Daddy again. I wondered how many fivers or tenners he would send this year. Mammy said we must forgive him because the war was on, but life was so hard without him.

* * *

There was a saying that if a hen crowed, it was a sign of bad luck. Well, one day, one of our hens came into the house and jumped into my youngest brother James's cot. It snuggled down in the warm covers, and when I threw it out into the yard it crowed like a cockerel - I was not the only witness. The next day James, just three years old, died

I heard Mammy blaming herself, and I felt guilty - I had thrown the hen out. The doctor said no-one was to blame - little James had died of pneumonia. But I think he could have been saved. Doctor Conway was called but didn't come until late the next night. It was dark. James was standing up in his cot holding the bars, crying and crying. He was very hot and wouldn't let anyone touch him. The doctor just told Mammy to boil the kettle and leave it boiling, move the cot near the fire and let the steam blow in little James's face. Mammy asked Doctor Conway what chances our brother had, and he replied "not much". He put some tablets on the table and left.

James died that night in Mammy's arms, while she begged him "please don't leave me".

All my life I have thought, why do we have hospitals? What are ambulances for? James could have been wrapped in blankets and driven to Dublin or Navan hospital in the back of the Doctor's car. But no matter how angry you get, you can't turn the clock back.

Poor James was laid out in his cot, with a penny on each eye to pay the ferryman for his journey to heaven. I was six. Seventy years ago, and I'm about to make a confession I've held onto my whole life.

LITTLE FECKER!

I stole the two pennies from James's eyes. Twice. A Mars Bar was four pence, so once wasn't enough. I immediately hated myself – for the theft but most of all for lying to Mammy. I almost choked on the Mars Bar – and I've hated myself for it since, even though Father Carberry forgave me when I confessed – three hail Marys and a promise never to steal again. This taught me a huge lesson about honesty that I've lived by for the rest of my life. You'll see that I may have stolen to keep the ones I love alive, but I can put my hand on my heart and say that after James's pennies, I never took anything for myself in the rest of my life.

Mammy was always coughing and she had started to lose weight. She would get breathless and tired but would still use all her energy to look after us all. One day it all got too much for her and she was taken to hospital.

My eldest sister Maureen had emigrated to England and lived near Daddy in Nuneaton, a mining town in Warwickshire. For the rest of us, as soon as we were able, we all had to find work or we'd starve. It was unusual then in Ireland for women to work outside the home, and if they did have jobs they usually lost them as soon as they married. But Rose got a job working for a doctor in Dublin, so Rita became responsible for the running of the house while Mammy was in hospital. She worked hard and kept us well fed. Benny, Vincie and Doney were working and, though wages were very poor, they were bringing in money to feed and clothe us.

Bringing Home the Bread... and the Wood!

Bread rationing had begun in 1942, and with no spuds in the garden out of season, there were hungry days. We weren't the only ones who suffered, nearly everyone who was out of "the know" went without bread. From memory it was rationed to less than a quarter of what we would normally eat. I remember fights over the last crusts in the bread cupboard, even if they had turned blue with mould.

Drastic action had to be taken. The delivery van turned up mid-week, and we would receive and pay for our ration of loaves. That was when Doney and I would sneak into the back of the lorry, a Bedford with two swing doors and a drop down back. If it wasn't raining the doors would be clipped back as there were a lot of deliveries to do, so Doney and I just climbed over the backboard. This had to be done with precision, exactly when the driver disappeared on the driver's side. You had to move quick to get behind the lorry and avoid being seen in the wing mirrors. Then, you couldn't jump on until he moved away to avoid vibration. It was easy for us though; we were like hungry rats.

The next move was to throw out sixteen loaves, two blocks of eight. This was another precision exercise – if the loaves landed on the road they'd be seen and taken within minutes, and if they landed in the ditch they'd be soaked with dirty water and useless. So we had to make sure they got past the ditch and into the field, quite a throw, and even then there was a risk they could be seen by a passing cyclist or pedestrian.

Then we had to wait until driver got to Sweeney's shop before we could jump off – by the time the driver got out and walked behind the back of his lorry we were in the back of the shop. The carefully planned looting was far from over – we now had to do the "hare's run" back, hoping and praying no-one had pinched our bread from the field. Often we'd get into the field and the exact location of the loaves was made obvious by the number of birds that had gathered - Doney and I would have made great scarecrows!

We did get caught, you see every loaf had to be accounted for and the only family that could eat another sixteen loaves on top of what they had already got was the Kellys. This meant another kick up the arse, though I don't remember any further punishment – I think perhaps the Garda sympathised with Mammy.

Survival was the name of the game – the fire had to be kept alive 24 hours a day for heating, and there was a lot of food to cook for the ten of us. Every night, Mammy would put the porridge on - a six gallon cast iron pot, which hung on a swinging bracket so you could position it over the fire and let the porridge simmer all night. Mammy would get up in the middle of the night to put logs and turf on the fire, turn the pot around, have a fag and a cough and go back to bed.

No-one could ever do porridge like our Mammy. She would cut it out of the pot with a big spoon, warm milk and sugar… our three poor dogs, which we used for catching rabbits and hares, would lie there thinking, "When are they going to stop eating, and give some to us?"

For many winters we suffered. Turf was expensive, coal was definitely a luxury so wood was always on the menu. Jock Woodruff was a friend of the family who would call for a cup of tea now and again. Jock was small but very strong, he had broken his back when in his late twenties which unfortunately gave him a hump. He worked and lived on a farm a few miles away.

One night we were all huddled around the fire which was hardly a fire and we didn't have another stick to put on it. Jock called in on the way to Sweeney's pub and could see how bad our situation was. Mammy was in hospital, Daddy was in England. Jock said he would call the next day and asked me to make sure that Benny and Vincie were home and also to make sure that Tom Traynor and his sons Davey and Joe were there.

As we all waited for Jock the next day, nobody knew why he had called the meeting or what was on his mind. But I had an idea, and I was right.

A few days earlier, I had been in the farmer's orchard when the farmer came up behind me and shouted, "Where's your friend?" He fired a twelve-bore shotgun into one of the apple trees, and Brendan Riley fell out of the tree next to it. For a minute I thought how lucky Brendan was, but he had broken bones in both his ankles. The farmer made me swear to say I'd never heard or seen a shot fired, and he took Brendan off to a Dublin hospital in his truck. The farmer's wife gave me a huge sack and said I could take as many apples as I could carry.

I kept my promise – I didn't tell anyone about the shotgun, until now, but I swore to make the farmer pay for what he'd done to Brendan with more than a few apples. I told Jock Woodruff that I had a plan: to cut down the farmer's big ash tree in the field, for firewood.

At the meeting, Jock explained that he had worked out exactly how we could pull off the plan. This would mean getting enough wood in one night to keep all of us warm for the rest of the winter.

It was December 1946, I had just had my tenth birthday, little did I know what we were in for. Five weeks later, one of the worst winters in history hit Ireland and the rest of the British Isles. It snowed so hard that the snow was higher than the hedgerows and we were on red alert for two months.

After Jock explained his plan, the Kellys and the Traynors met next day. The tree was 200 yards from our house, a medium sized ash about fifty feet high with a three-foot wide trunk. Jock guessed it would produce about two tons of wood.

I couldn't believe he was actually going to steal it – I had seen how violently the local farmer reacted if you stole an apple. If he caught us stealing a whole tree I thought he'd probably kill us all. Jock's plan involved starting as soon as it got dark the next evening and working right through the night. We got together all of the old carbine lamps we could find, and our main weapons of attack were three big cross cut saws – six feet long, operated by two people, one at each end. On top of that we had a pile of various hand saws and half a dozen axes – more tools than hands. For transport the Traynors had a solid wheeled flat-bed truck and between us we found four wheelbarrows.

We had a large corrugated iron shed in our garden so the first job was to clear that to make room for the tree – it had to disappear somewhere.

The night of the disappearing tree is an excited blur in my mind. I was only ten, but I insisted on being part of the "gang". Jock put me on watch - I remember the sawing seemed so loud that surely someone would hear and come to stop us. But in hindsight we were a long way from the farm itself and from any other home. I soon got bored, and jealous of my brothers and friends having all the fun with the big saws. I left my post and went to carry twigs and branches from the downed tree to the truck and barrows.

I must have fallen asleep in the field, because by the next day, most of the tree was in our shed. The stump, standing up about three foot high, was still in the ground and the next day we camouflaged it with muck and old leaves before daylight.

A few weeks later the farmer's manager Paddy Greoghan called at the house to visit Mammy, who was out of hospital. He said to her, "You know, Julia, you've got a lovely view from the kitchen window here. Ah, sure, it's a view from here like I've never seen before. I could have sworn there was a big ash tree just up there by the hedge." He winked, threw his leg over his bike and grinned as he rode away.

And yes, the tree did disappear twice. Once from the hedgerow… and then up the chimney!

Though it's hard to condone theft, I forgive myself because the winter that followed – in January 1947 – was one of the worst on record. Snow was over the hedges, and it was freezing for months. I really do believe that without the old farmer's ash tree the Kellys could have frozen to death that winter.

I pride myself on being honest, but looking back there were times when the whole family sat around the table with no food, so I felt I had no choice but to "borrow" those loaves, or a few spuds from the farmer's field. Stealing spuds was a challenge, I did it in such a way that the farmer would never be able to tell he'd been robbed. With a small spade I would dig under the potato stalk, careful not to disturb it, scrape the soil away, take four or six spuds, replace the soil carefully and move along to another area. I would do this until I could barely lift the sack. The journey back from the farm with a sack of spuds over my shoulder was always scary, but I didn't do it often.

Father Carberry always found out. We were good Catholics; we would eat the spuds then tell him at confession. Somehow, at that young age, without telling me that stealing was all right, Father Carberry made me feel that I could put right the wrong I had done. I hope I have proved him right and to a certain extent made up for these discretions by being generous whenever I could in later life.

One day on a spade trip I sunk the spade into some soft soil and the soil started to move. I was scared but curious, worried that I may have hit a wasps' nest and I had heard that wasps in a frenzy could kill you. In a bit of a panic I walloped the moving ground with my spade, I should have run away but I was frozen to the spot. When the movement stopped, I scraped away a bit of soil and was horrified to find that I had hit a cuddly little rabbit. I felt sick but this was about survival and we had rabbit stew.

If we had enough money, we'd go food shopping in Dublin. I remember one hot Saturday, I got a lift from Jock, who let me put all the groceries on his flat bed truck. When we got back to Kilbride, he missed our turn and carried on down to Sweeney's pub. I had not long been confirmed, so I had taken the pledge not to take a drink until I was 18. Well, every time I swigged down a bottle of stout, another one replaced it. A man jumped off his bike and ran into the pub, shouting at Jock, I think your lorry has a leak! Jock went out and came back looking very sad, he said "your butter's run off". That was only a small part of the problem. When I got home tiddly and with no butter, Rita caught me. I was reported first to my Aunt Rosie and then to Father Carberry for drinking and breaking the pledge. I had to say ten week's Hail Marys as penance.

LITTLE FECKER!

With my sister Rose at my confirmation

Religion played a large part in my childhood and Sunday mass was the highlight of the week. Everyone seemed to be there, those who were missing had to have a good reason. When I was very ill after I had my tonsils out I missed school and at least two Sunday masses, when I returned to school I was branded a *pagan*. So you were expected to be at mass even if you had to crawl there.

Me and the lads always sat near the back of the chapel, last in first out. The men who loved a pint of Guinness always sat on the back seats too.

There were very rich people went to our chapel. One Sunday the wooden collection plate was going back and forward between seats. I nudged Sean when I saw a white fiver sort of unravelling itself. The donor must have had it screwed up in his hand. Anyway the plate turned the corner, I noticed when it got to me the fiver had gone. It was not hard to work out – Sean went to Sweeney's shop and bought us all a Mars bar and a bottle of lemonade, I thought no, it couldn't be him, he didn't even swear!

While we danced on the precipice of poverty in Kilbride, we did have family who lived "in the city", who were better off. On Daddy's side of the family, Aunt Kathy had a beautiful home in Brunswick Street in the centre of Dublin, and her two sons were doing very well – one had a transport business and the other worked as a scientist in America. The Maloneys – Mammy's sister Cissie, Nick, Jack, Butty and Rosie lived off the Phibsborough Road in Dublin. They were great people, and we got to stay with them sometimes, at weekends or in the holidays, to give Mammy a break. There was always a nice meal and a warm welcome. Jack was a great footballer, and had trials with Manchester United and Aston Villa, but came home because he missed Dublin and the family.

Aunt Cissie was an absolute gem, everyone loved her. I sometimes got to go and visit, and stay over - being in Dublin was magic, compared with the quiet of home, I'd get to sell newspapers off O'Connell Street and work on a fruit stall on Moore Street market

LITTLE FECKER!

School and Other Scrapes

School was strict. And while Mammy was grateful for the food my brother Doney and I would bring home, she knew what was going on. I thought she'd believe me when I said, "Mammy, I found *another* loaf of bread on my way home from school." But Mammy had more concern for my long-term welfare than our short-term hunger, so she'd collude with the priests to make sure I attended school as often as they could make me.

Of course, the only way they could make sure I got to school was if Father Murphy himself came to fetch me. But the priest could only come himself about once a week. He would call at the house in his black Austin car, and take us directly to school.

The headmaster, Mr Callaghan, would stand me at the top of the classroom, facing all the other boys and girls, with Father Murphy still in attendance, steely-eyed, at the back. Mr Callaghan would hand me his penknife and send me out into the grounds to cut a stick from one of the trees. While I was gone, the class would receive a lecture on the evil of missing school. From experience, I knew that I had to be quick. I also knew that if the stick wasn't at least 2 feet 6 inches long, and half an inch thick, he would send me out again and I'd be punished further for having wasted his valuable time. On my return he would take back his knife, stand beside me and painstakingly, almost lovingly, clean all the small twigs from the stick. I would look into the eyes of fifty classmates, and see worry from the girls (I'd smile and wink when I was sure Father Murphy wouldn't see), and smugness from the boys, hiding their relief that the stick wasn't destined for *their* backside!

To add to my humiliation and to prolong the waiting, Mr Callaghan would order me to pick up the rubbish he had made, which required me to bend over. Bent double, with two handfuls of twigs, I knew what was coming; one lash for each day missed. As Father Murphy only came for me once a week, this usually meant four or five lashes.

So I became used to pain, discipline and justice at an early age. And as long as I could see what was causing it, and why, then I could cope with any amount of pain.

The whole experience was fascinating. I understood why I was being punished – missing school was wrong, Mr Callaghan had to show who was boss. The pain was never a disincentive – the benefit of providing food for my Mammy, brothers and sisters could not be outweighed. And I always got a thrill from seeing the range of reactions on those fifty faces – my first "audience".

Callaghan was a strict disciplinarian and I suppose, thinking back, he was a good teacher. But when you're frightened then fear means you tend not to listen, and if you don't listen you don't learn. School was tough; Catholicism, catechism and holy water. Now I have no problem with religion, but the powers that be in Ireland should have known better, and more concentration should have been put into making sure their people could read, write and spell. Not least, this would have made it easier to learn their religion!

Let's just say that as I write this, I'm grateful someone else will be checking my spelling and grammar!

I was lashed for playing truant - mitching - and for not learning the religion. Mr Callaghan would keep us back after school; on one disciplinary stay-over there were five of us and he asked us questions. If we got it wrong, we got a lash from a three-tailed leather strap for each syllable of the right answer! Lord help us if the answer was a long one! We were so nervous that we would get the simplest question wrong. Noel Sullivan got an eight-syllable answer wrong. On about the sixth lash Noel jerked his hand as the strap came down, Callaghan hit the back of his own hand, the strap caught his fingers and ripped one of his nails clean off. There was blood everywhere. But no-one laughed, we just stood, silent. Callaghan calmly put his hand in his pocket and pulled out a large white handkerchief. Wrapping up his hand, he said "Lessons are over, go home".

The incident didn't change Callaghan, just his method. The strap was replaced by a big stick, as thick as your forefinger and two feet long. One of the lads, Sean Bruton, was first to experience the pain of the ash plant, with five lashes. Half an hour later he got another question wrong, and his hand was already red raw. I was amazed at what happened next.

As the first of six lashes came down, Sean caught the stick, dispossessed Callaghan of his lethal weapon, broke it in two and threw it in the open fire. Again, Callaghan, who was past retirement age and semi-crippled with a poorly leg, calmly said, "Lessons over, go home". Somewhere inside this figure there was a kind heart.

Another teacher never to forget was Biddy Maguire, she'd belt you as soon as look at you. One warm day we were out on the steps, trying our best to learn something, when Biddy decided to start beating my brother Doney on the head. Doney had enough, stuck the boot on her shin and ran. It must have been sore because she went down on one knee roaring "Get him! Get him!" We all looked on, we were only kids. She went to the senior side of the school, picked out the three biggest lads she could find, and sent them like a pack of wolves to go and get Doney. I can still picture my brother running at full speed up the road, head going from side to side, they hadn't a cat in hell's chance of catching him!

And then there was The Crow - Mr Crow – a Christian Brother who temporarily replaced Mr Callaghan, after the head injured himself falling off his bike into a ditch. Now this man Crow was a nutter! He was 6'2" tall, and stalked up and down the classroom in a big black brotherhood gown. It used to frighten the shite out of me just to hear his footsteps coming up from behind.

One day Snowy, one of the big lads, had his head down, "working". When I say big lad, these fellas had

LITTLE FECKER!

left school, but if after a year they hadn't got a job they had to come back. You can imagine how interested they were in studying. Crow leaned over Snowy, nicknamed for of his very blond, crew-cut hair, to inspect the progress of his composition. Snowy had not even started - instead he had drawn a beautifully artistic replica of a crow. The teacher picked up a triple-decker wooden pencil box and smashed it over Snowy's head, knocking him to the floor. There were pens, pencils and rubbers flying everywhere. Snowy never came back.

On another occasion, Crow beat up a lad called Frank Corcoran. Not with a stick - he used his knuckles. Now Frank's dad was a wiry man, not very big, he always wore a black hat. He was hard of hearing, but a brilliant lip reader. I wasn't about to say anything to him or about him! When he heard that his son got a hiding from Crow, he came to the school to enquire. He walked into the classroom, straight up to Crow and, silent and expressionless, flattened him with one punch. We loved it! Especially when the rest of the lessons were cancelled. We were free for the day!

I left school when I was twelve; having to help provide for a family with nine children, and a father absent overseas, was a great excuse. Not that I attended school much before the age of twelve, mitching was more important - time out to work - in the fields, on the thrashing machines, on a market stall, or selling newspapers in O'Connell Street – time to make money for food.

* * *

Education is a luxury. No amount of education is any good if you are dead from starvation. Most lads are adventurous, brave, daring, looking for a challenge round every corner. While we did our fair share of scrapping at school, there were many more hazardous trials to experience. By the law of averages I reckon I should have died at least twice by the time I was 14.

Once I was swinging on a branch over a brook. The water was flowing fast after two days of heavy storms. The branch broke and I fell in. I struggled to get to the surface, and when I did break free of the cold water I was under this big roll of barbed wire, there to prevent anyone from getting into the Den River, which ran across the brook.

Noel Traynor ran for help, so I was on my own. In front of me the brook, behind me the raging river, forty feet wide, seventy feet deep. I couldn't hang on, and I couldn't swim. In a situation like that, I think you come to accept the situation and fear leaves you. My head popped above the water in the middle of the river and all I could see was a whirlpool. The water was moving so fast, I started to drift under the bridge, but somehow managed to keep my head above water.

Something gave me the strength to make a mad dash for the bank. Doggy paddling, I got to the bank, and dragged myself through briars and thorns to safety.

People appeared from everywhere, as if they'd stood by to watch my brave escape before coming to congratulate me. My arms were covered in blood and my lungs were ready to burst, but I was Mammy's big

LITTLE FECKER!

favourite that day. Everyone wanted to love me, I was treated as a hero instead of the stupid prat that I was.

Only a few hundred yards from that river, just off the path between home and the shops, was a very deep well – Rooks Cross Well. Guess who fell into it. Rose and I went to Sweeney's for some groceries and had forgotten to take a shopping bag, so we stuffed the food in our pockets. It was very cold, so I had a big heavy old black overcoat on. I stuffed about 3lbs of butter and a couple of bags of sugar into the pockets, so you can imagine when I fell in the well feet first I went down like a bag of cement.

Despite the heavy coat and its heavier cargo I somehow drifted back up far enough for Rose to grab my collar and help me out. There's no doubt she saved my life against the odds – perhaps I wasn't meant to die just yet.

I decided to teach myself to swim - in probably the most dangerous quarry in the country. There were ridges and underwater paths and you had to know exactly where they were if you weren't a good swimmer. I was soon in trouble, and this time I was frightened, very frightened. I started to kick and deadly, sticky vines wrapped round my ankles. The more I tugged, the tighter they got, and I couldn't break them. I could see stars, my head was pounding, I was losing consciousness. The next thing I knew I was floating, supported by a big hand under my chin. Tom Traynor, a tall, powerful man, saved my life, he had dived down and cut the water vines from my legs with his penknife. Tom and his lovely family, four sons and a daughter; Tommy, Davy, Jo, Noel and Rose, were my great friends.

One day Doney and I decided it would be fun to walk on the iced-over river. It was a lovely feeling to walk on water, we joked that it must have been nice also for the good Lord, to do it without the ice. He must have been with me that day, because as we walked slowly, a high-pitched pinging sound surrounded us as the ice cracked. We walked quicker, looking for a gap in the thick bushes on either side of the river. But the faster we went, the farther the crack raced ahead, suddenly splitting in a V right in front of us.

I lurched as I felt the ice give way under our weight. Still there was no gap on either bank, so I decided we had to take our chance with the bushes. I grabbed Doney's hand and dived, and as I lay on my back on top of a spiky bramble I saw a crack in the ice open and close within just a few seconds, exactly where we'd been standing. It would have been certain death – Doney and I would have been under that ice with no-one knowing we'd ever been there. Once again the Good Lord put his hand out to help us that day!

I lost a few friends to accidents. One fell off the top of a load of hay and died. Another was riding his bike in a storm when high winds blew a tree down and killed him. I often wonder why were they there at that time, maybe the Lord needed to take some young ones to accompany some of the elderly who die.

One day I was walking with my brother Pat, three years younger than me. Two miles from home, we climbed over a high gate into an enclosed high-walled garden, looking for chunks of wood or anything else useful. Suddenly a man was standing behind us – we recognised him, he was known as the "tanner man" because he would sell bric-a-brac from door to door and give sixpences to the children. He was big, over six feet tall, he had ridden up on his bike and climbed into the garden. We had never heard of gay people or paedophiles, so although he startled us we had no particular reason to be frightened.

He complimented us on how fit we looked, and said he would give us a chance to prove how strong we were. He lay flat on his back and invited me to sit across his stomach, and lean forward holding his wrists. He asked me to push on his wrists to pin him down, and allowed me to push his arms until the backs of his hands were touching the ground. By this time our faces were almost touching. I noticed he was shaking and he said I was very strong, as he couldn't lift either of his arms. Then he said, with a funny grin on his face, "It's my turn".

I didn't like the look in his eyes and said I wanted to go now. He said, "No, not till I know how strong you really are". He pushed me on my back, held my wrists and gently pushed my arms back until they were hard on the ground. He was moving his body in a funny way - when I think back I suppose his groin would have been in between my knees. He said "Now I want you to lift your right arm and I will try and hold you down". He said, "Come on, come on". I lifted as hard as I could, and he eased off a bit, saying,

"I told you – you're stronger than me!" He was shaking all over, and sweat was running down his face. I looked at Pat and shouted "Get over the gate!" I twisted and pushed, and somehow managed to get free – I think the man let go of me and this was all part of his game. Pat was halfway up the gate. I could hardly walk, I felt so weak. When I got to the gate, Pat was already on top. I started to drag myself up but froze; my shoulder and arm muscles were completely shot from the effort of showing how strong I was – a clever game! I couldn't move one way or the other. The tanner man was getting up - I thought I was about to die.

But he got to me, stopped, pulled out some change and gave Pat and me a tanner each. Then he jumped over the wall, strolled to his bike and rode away. I've been haunted all my life by that experience. Pat and I have never talked about it. Pat being younger may not have understood the danger until I told him to get over the gate. I was more worried for him than for myself.

Doney and I were in one or two close shaves, I remember the Garda calling at the house one day to pick both of us up. I thought our mitching days were over, Artain here we come. Artain was a special school for boys who had poor attendance records or who didn't go to school at all. Your sentence was two years with no appeal. I often wondered if I would have been better off, quite a few of my pals went in and some of them did very well in life, at least they had an education of sorts and were very streetwise.

LITTLE FECKER!

As the Garda were reading something to Mammy, Doney looked at me, gestured with his head towards the door and shot past the two Garda. I shot the other side, and by the time they turned round we were on the road.

They came after us, two big men and very fit but knowing our ground was to our advantage. No-one could go over a five bar gate quicker than Doney and me, it was still rattling when they got to it and we were half way across the 14 acre field. All we could hear was them shouting "We'll be back for you, you little feckers".

Mammy wasn't happy about it and really told us off - I remember standing in the middle of the floor and shouting "Feck". I turned and ran; it was the only time I ever swore in front of Mammy.

I was away for hours, afraid for my life to go back as it got dark. Mammy got worried and told all the family to look for me. I could hear them all shouting "Noel! Ned! Mammy says it's alright now, you can come home for dinner!"

When I got into the house she simply put her hands around the back of my head and caressed me, saying, "It's alright son, now sit and have your dinner." It was strange, and hard work sitting on my own eating with a family audience.

I have always cherished that forgiving, loving moment; it must have been very difficult for Mammy to split her love up ten different ways.

I had my tonsils out in the Navan hospital and I thought I was going to die again. The big nurse gave me a bollocking because I had spots on my back. "We don't like kids with spots in this hospital" she snorted. How the feck am I supposed to know I've got spots on me back? I'm dying of a sore throat and all she can go on about is me back! Anyway, she whipped my clothes off then pulled this great big nightshirt over me head – it was big enough to fit Joe Louis. She gave me half a glass of ether – horrible stuff, highly flammable – if you had a fag at the same time you'd go through the roof like a rocket!

The next I knew I was staring up at the surgeon, mid-operation. The nurse slammed a gas mask over my face. When I woke up again, I felt so sick. I could taste the ether and was dizzy from the gas. I wasn't happy with the operation because I had been a good singer, in the choir when I went to school. But my singing days were over; they replaced my glands with gravel.

Worse was to come – I picked up a throat infection from the op. I couldn't eat or drink, Mammy didn't know what to do, I was so thin you could have locked the door with me. Aunt Rosie, a lot of experience in the nursing, boiled two eggs, mashed them with butter in a cup and sat with me till I was finished. She was a lovely woman, our Aunt Rosie.

Once I had an abscess the size of a duck's egg on the back of my neck. I walked round with my head at 45 degrees, until Rosie was called, a pre-planned secret operation.

LITTLE FECKER!

I went to get a drink from the tap, and the enamel basin was full of boiling water. Something was going on – we didn't leave hot water lying around to go cold! I had no clue as to what was going to happen.

My brothers, Benny and Vincie, grabbed me from behind, Rita grabbed my hair and they all held me over the boiling basin. Rosie stepped up with a scalpel and carved the abscess out like a hot cross bun. It was a frightening sight in the bowl, blood everywhere - I still have the scar on the back of my neck and often wonder what would have happened without Rosie's intervention – I might have grown another head!

One of my most painful experiences came when a farmer swung a hammer at an annoying seagull and managed to hit it, injuring it badly. He told two of the lads to put it out of its misery. They grabbed a wing each to carry it, and started swinging it backwards and forwards. It was making a hell of a racket. They swung it towards me and it lashed out, its beak caught me right in the bollocks and it wouldn't let go!

I've never felt physical pain like it! I still flinch whenever I hear a seagull squawk - perhaps I'm lucky that Daddy decided to settle as far from the sea as he could get when he arrived in England!

And there were events that stick with me to this day, simply because I still carry the physical scars. One day Vincie was cutting down a 20 ft tree. At the last minute, he shouted at me to move out of the way. But I managed to move into the way. The tree hit me smack on the top of my head knocked me out. I still have the bump.

On another occasion I was on a playground swing when Sean Bruton twisted one of the chains so I spun round and round. Sean wasn't a boy to do anything in half measures – I spun so fast that I flew out of the swing and was knocked out on the concrete. Another small facial scar for the collection.

Somebody kicked me up the arse on a football pitch one day. If he'd done it in the street I'd probably have knocked him out, but this was sport, so somehow it was allowed and accepted. I still have coccyx problems to this day.

But fighting was part and parcel of any normal week. A bunch of brothers called the Sullivans, who went on to become top level Gaelic footballers in County Meath, made a hobby of getting into scraps regularly. If you didn't get into fights of your own accord, the Sullivans would arrange fights for you. They were quite methodical, no one missed out - I often wondered if they kept an official rota.

Once they made me fight my mate Owen at school. Friends were often set against each other like this, and there was no option but to fight properly. I beat Owen, and there was blood everywhere. I ran off and hid behind a tree and cried – it hurt me so much to cause pain to a good friend.

Work

From an academic point of view, school had been a waste of time. I learned to read and write, but do neither well. I learned a bit of arithmetic later, when I set up in business and had to make sure I covered costs (and when I needed to check the bookmaker wasn't cheating me out of my winnings!).

In the autumn of my thirteenth year I decided I'd had enough schooling, and I joined a combined harvester gang, a bunch of men who owned shares in a combined harvester and would sub-contract to farmers who didn't have one.

Because I was so young I wasn't allowed anywhere near the dangerous moving parts, so I was given the job of chaffing out. I quickly learned that there was a certain amount of skill – you had to estimate the size of the "rick" in order to calculate the space you were going to need, if you cocked up with no space the mill may be forced to stop. The harvester must not stop at any cost - that meant a kick up the arse and no job – no pay either.

It happened to me on one farm, three days of solid thrashing, the men working like machines to keep up with the machine; dust, flies and sweat, rats by the dozen. On the third day I was in trouble and needed help to pull back the mountain of chaff. Because of that the farmer refused to pay me. I cried in the repair shop out of sight until one of the lads came in and gave me 2/6d and said sorry that he hadn't helped me earlier. It wasn't really his responsibility and I really didn't want to take his money, but again it was food on our table, so I thanked him and left.

I was so angry with the farmer that I picked up two big holdalls, filled them with every tool I could lay my hands on, hooked them on the handlebars of my bike and off I went. A mile down the road I came to a deep pond. The tools are probably still in that pond, it cost that miserable farmer dear for cheating me. I cried again when I told my mammy, who was very ill in bed – after all the money was for her, to get food and stuff to keep the house going.

I got a contract away from home; long shifts, 7am til 8pm, then the gang would be off to the nearest pub, twelve pints of stout in two hours and come back well oiled. They were big strong men who would fight at the drop of a hat - I felt quite frightened at times and pretended to be asleep. After a while it would go quiet except for the snoring and farting.

There were four in the caravan I slept in, two double bunks, me in the bottom bunk so I could get out quietly and get the breakfast started, sausages, eggs and bacon. I'd have the pan too hot – the cry would go out: "the sausages are bursting all over the pan!" Tempers would fly: "Ned you're a little bollox, can't you fry a fecking sausage without bursting it?"

But sleeping on the bottom bunk had its disadvantages. One night I woke from a splendid dream with a lovely warm feeling – the man in the bunk above had decided to relieve his bladder of four pints of Guinness, no longer black and white but yellowy green – over my back. I had no option but to remain quiet – a wet blanket is better than a bloody nose!

I had various jobs, one was at a great business, Jackie May's little supermarket, my job was to weigh the various meals, from porridge oats to linseed. I was busy every hour of every day, there was good luck and bad luck to be had – the good luck was getting to virtually rear six piglets to become prize pigs. Jackie, a real gentleman, was over the moon, he gave me extra money and a big bag of groceries. Everyone was happy until disaster struck – I gave the wrong meal to a dear old lady one day and her calf died.

There were no groceries on the handlebars of my bike that day. I grew up quite a bit in that journey home. I knew I had let the family down. Sacked, my confidence was gone. There had been twenty lads after that job, and I had got it because I was a son of Mammy Kelly. I was so disappointed with myself. But you have to learn from your mistakes.

I got a short term job as a cattle driver, 13½ years old and on my own, I used to go to the railway station when all the wild heifers were unloaded. Down from the Dublin and Kerry mountains, they were wild. I drove between fifty and seventy at a time, straight over Carl's Bridge and out into the country roads. I lost three in the river one day; conditions on the trains were rough and they were desperate for water - I can still see them swimming. Hopefully they got out somewhere. The survivors were driven hard, with me shouting and cracking a home-made leather whip, the 17 miles to Ratoath.

Working on farms I often saw horses being overworked. Once one of my favourites, a big shire, was harnessed to a cart carrying far too much hay, stuck in the mud. The big horse couldn't move the load, so the farmer got a handful of hay, set fire to it and threw it under the horse's belly. I ran away, unable to watch. The next day the horse was gone.

On another occasion I watched a shire walk up and down a track in the field, non-stop for several days. When I asked why he had done this, I was told "He's dying from a broken heart. Overworked, he will keep walking till he drops."

I loved horses and still do. I wanted to be a jockey, so I went to work for Charlie Rogers at his stables, a fair old cycle ride from home. I really enjoyed my time there, they had a big cattle herd, and I used to get on a horse to get the cattle in.

As soon as the cattle saw me on the horse they knew it was milking time and they would start heading across the fields towards the milking sheds. The farm had just got new-fangled milking machines – I thought it was a shame when the machines came in because I used to love it when the old fellers would squirt warm milk in your face and into your mouth. On the positive side, though, also gone were the days when the cow would pick up its hind leg and put its foot straight into the bucket. (They always seemed to wait until the bucket was full – how did they know?)

I worked for Jimmy Parkinson, milking at 6am: full bucket, cow's foot and half a leg in three gallons of milk. I shouted Jimmy, "How do I get his fecking leg out of the bucket?" Jimmy said "without spilling the fecking milk, or you're sacked!" It wasn't long before I moved from milking cows to breaking horses!

One day I was on a wild two year old. He had hardly been broken, and horses are clever – they suss you out in a minute. You have to take charge or they just ignore you. I was a little soft at the time and I had no whip, so as I got towards the cattle he just stopped and started to graze. I slapped and kicked him, but he just carried on grazing, as if to say, "feck you, I'm hungry". I got off – I had no option, even though I knew I would struggle to get back on, and that was it – he bolted! I now had to get the cattle back manually.

They didn't take much notice of me without the horse, so it wasn't easy. I wasn't looking forward to a bollocking for getting the cattle back late. Then out of the blue two of the lads came flying across the field on horseback, they were pleased to see I was OK as my horse had arrived back without me, so it wasn't such a bad day and I learnt a little bit about horses.

I had another hair-raising experience at Rogers's stables. The lads there would risk their lives to break in the two-year-olds. These horses were wild, they would kick your head off given the chance. It was great entertainment!

Watching one day, Sean Gilbert asked me to ride this horse out and train him for an hour. He assured me the horse was well broken so on I got. The horse took off like a rocket – we flew across the field at 35 miles an hour, I said goodbye to me brothers, sisters and Mammy and hello to God, I hope you're expecting me! The horse headed for the vegetation plant, I thought this would slow him down and the fall wouldn't be so hard, but I had forgotten the electric fence that separated the vegetation from the grazing field! The horse saw the fence though, and pulled up so fast that I took off, landing on top of the fence! I was jumping about like an electric eel, a shocking experience!

I was spending a long time every day in the saddle, getting the hang of the horses and relishing the riding, especially at a gallop. I had no fear when it came to pushing a horse to run as fast as it could – boy it was exhilarating! Rogers trained horses for racing, and he was happy to let me pursue my dream of becoming a jockey for quite a few months. But one morning he came to me and said, "forget the idea of becoming a jockey, young Ned. It's a shame, you're a good rider, but you're the wrong build. I reckon you'll struggle to hold your weight, you might as well give up now, not waste any more of your time."

I was gutted – I had always just worked at whatever came along, just to make a few pounds to help feed the family, and I had never thought beyond that to a career. But in that single comment Rogers created, and simultaneously destroyed – a dream: all of a sudden I could see the satisfying, glamorous and well-paid life of a jockey ahead. Then it was gone. I struggled to accept Mr Rogers's view that I would be too big. Too big? I was just a whippersnapper!

LITTLE FECKER!

Angry with Rogers, I challenged him to prove how he could possibly tell. He said nothing, just grabbed my arm with his big right hand, forming a ring between his thumb and middle finger, which met quite easily around my scrawny wrist. He grunted and pulled a dissatisfied face, and I felt for a second that I had won, but Rogers bent quickly and did the same with my right ankle, knocking me off balance and almost sending me flying. "Yes, the wrong build *and* heavy boned with it. The bones never lie, son. You're a small boy, but you'll be a big man."

I fought back tears of frustration as I left the yard that day – how could I argue, how could I prove that he was wrong, had to be wrong? Truth was, I couldn't. Mr Rogers was an expert, and of course he turned out to be right.

Some years later my eldest son Sean got married in Newcastle, on the day of a big race meeting in the city. On the night before, most of the country's top flat jockeys were staying in our hotel, and I spoke to several of them – including Walter Swinburne. They were real gentleman, but I couldn't fail to see the smile in their eyes when I told them I had once held hopes of becoming a jockey! I laughed out loud when I got back to my room and jumped on the weighing scales - they tipped 16 stones!

The next job was back to milking cows, feeding, scrubbing and cooking for two farmer brothers, Micky and Jack Newman. Neither had married, both worked all day every day, and I never saw either touch a drink or cigarette.

The Newmans had a magnificent cock turkey, massive when it was in full plumage. I went to work in a red jacket one morning – it probably belonged to one of my sisters. Without warning the turkey landed on my back, its claws tearing into me. I managed to get the thing off, and I was so scared that I ran off across the field. The turkey folded away its beautiful plumage and took off after me, and boy could he run – he caught up with me in seconds and out came his plumage again! I fought off his second attack more aggressively and he gave up, but I was taking no chances – I avoided him the rest of that day.

"I told you never to wear red!" smirked Jack. Lying bastard. I dyed the jacket black that night, and the next day the cock took no notice of me whatsoever.

One day the brothers fell out in the yard. Micky took a woman in - locals say she was from Dublin, looking to make a few bob. She was a lot younger than Micky but she did work hard. Jack was tossing some straw into a calf pen with his two-pronged fork when the argument started. He jabbed the fork at Micky's face, and took his left eye out of his socket. Micky screamed, Jack fell to his knees, a broken man.

I ran for help as fast as I could, vomiting as I ran. I flagged down a car, the driver got help. Micky survived, and the brothers carried on working the farm together after he recovered, but I never went back.

One small contract, one twelve hour shift, dawn till dusk, was a punctuation mark in my life. Just twelve

LITTLE FECKER!

hours, no way would they stop the old "traction machine". It was a nice day and had gone well - with just one full-sized rick to go, chaff was beginning to pile up around me, so I threw down my rake and borrowed the farmer's four-pronged fork. I was warned at all costs to look after this prize fork – three generations old, shaft like porcelain, light as a feather. I forked like mad to clear my space, and carefully put the fork to one side while I dragged away the chaff.

Two feet from the bottom of the rick we knew what to expect – rats. They would start off bolting one at a time, then in threes and fours, as we got nearer the bottom of the rick, the rats knew their time was up – they'd have to find new digs! We tied our trouser bottoms with twine to stop the rats shooting up our trouser legs. They were big and nasty, they came for you on hind legs squealing like banshees on fire.

I had the fork in my hand when one came for me – "whack!" I missed the rat and smashed the prize fork in two. "Shag this," I thought, "he'll kill me!" I pushed the two bits back together and I couldn't believe it – it went together perfectly and looked like new. My brain was working like mad, everyone was tidying up at the end of the job, I quickly leaned the fork against the wall of the farmer's house.

I don't think I've ever been so scared in all my life as when I saw the queue to get paid that day. Worse still, I was last in the queue, it was dark and I had five miles of dark lanes to encounter on my own, dead battery in the flash lamp, money or no money, sore arse or no sore arse, I was going to have to get home.

I thought to myself "if I'm lucky I'll get a quid, if I'm unlucky I won't be able to sit on the saddle of me bike all the way home". I got to the front of the queue, fearing the worst. I couldn't believe what happened. The farmer shoved £2 10s in my hand! For one day's work and a broken fork!

I took the money, feeling guilty and excited as I pushed me bike out into the dark lane. The farmer shouted after me "I know you broke me fecking prize fork you little whore! Anyways, God bless you and look after your dear Mammy!"

I didn't cry till I was home in Mammy's bedroom – I couldn't wait to tell her about the money, especially after the previous disaster. I tried to hand her the £2 10s, she looked at it but didn't take it – instead she squeezed my hand and said "keep that for yourself, buy yourself a new coat." I looked up into her eyes – I'd never had a new anything, let alone a coat. "I know, Noel" she said, "I know."

Goodbye Mammy

Deep down I knew something was wrong. I have never forgotten her eyes, the way she looked at me – a long, fond "wish you well" look that I have shed many a tear over since that day. I firmly believe that with those words and that look from a mother to her thirteen-year-old son she pointed the way for me to go out into the world and be a go-getter.

I only ever remember poor Mammy with bad health. One time she went to hospital and was in for a good few weeks – when she came out she had put on weight and looked really healthy, but she must have had TB because she was soon ill again. It had never stopped her from looking after us. Then, after years of looking after the family, one day she just took to her bed, and never got out.

Mammy was very ill now. Daddy was sent for. Maureen, my eldest sister flew home from England. Mammy was making the same noise as Granny did when she was dying. At 13, I don't think you really take it on board. Part of your system tells you this is not happening, you refuse to believe you won't see your Mammy alive again. I was in and out of the bedroom; Rita and Rose trying to comfort Mammy. The clock stopped at 2pm; the agonising rattling in Mammy's chest also stopped. Rita and Rose were crying out loud. The tears ran down my face like a stream. Like they are while I'm trying to write this down.

Mammy was only 47. I was told to go and meet Bernie and Pat coming from school to tell them that Mammy was dead. I can still see the blank shock on their faces. Bernie was only 10 and Pat 11. The whole family was in shock and friends and neighbours couldn't believe it.

At the wake, the day before the funeral, Mammy was in her coffin in the bedroom. People came from all over. "Very sad about your loss" they said. It was like a drama, something that had been written, but not something you rehearsed, you just went through the motions.

I had a blister on my hand from pulling corks and whipping tops off Guinness bottles. There seemed to be hundreds of bottles drunk. People were singing and dancing, which seemed really strange to me; why were they not all sad like me for losing Mammy? Maureen saw me getting angrier and angrier as I started to rip the bottle tops off and almost throw the Guinness bottles into outstretched hands.

"What's wrong, Ned?" She asked, taking me by the shoulders and looking deep into my eyes, with the same caring look that Mammy used to give me.

"Look at them! They don't care that Mammy's dead!"

"Of course they do! They're celebrating her life, how wonderful she was, and how happy she'll be in heaven!" Instantly, I felt stupid, like I was the one letting Mammy down now.

"So, do you have a smile for Mammy?" Maureen asked. I smiled, hugged her and went back to opening the bottles with a big grin on my face. I smiled until I collapsed exhausted at the end of a very long night.

At the funeral the next day, there was a huge turnout. The coffin was to be carried to the beautiful big church in Kilbride, with its small graveyard. It was a fine day, and I was really happy for Mammy. Then, as we were leaving the house, I overheard someone say, "such a shame. When it doesn't rain at a burial, the deceased won't be happy in heaven." The Irish are known as a superstitious race, but I didn't question the validity of the comment. It threw me into the

LITTLE FECKER!

deepest despair – the thought of Mammy, who had suffered so much in her life, and given so much for all of us so that we could be as happy as possible, not to be happy for the rest of eternity?

I cried all the way to the church, and all through the service. My stomach ached as I saw they were about to lower her into the grave - couldn't they see what they were doing? I wanted to stop them, make them wait until it was raining. Then, just as Mammy was lowered into the grave, it started raining. "Yes!". The rain made me feel better - if anyone deserved happiness forever in heaven, it was Mammy.

I often think of Mammy. You would have a job to find a closer family – years of standing by one another with Daddy away and Mammy in and out of hospital, ten visits to have babies, then with TB and then ill for quite some time with what we now believe was cancer, a tragic end for a princess. Mammy taught me the most important things in the world; to be civil, kind, and well-mannered. She taught me how it was so important to say 'thank you', and how, where and why to do so. Mammy made it easy to be grateful for everything, even if it was already ours. I would work twelve hours on the thrashing machine for a quid and although I had worked my little bollocks off for it, I always said thank you. Good manners. Everyone said, "These kids are well brought up, even if they have nothing". God bless Mammy, you were an angel on Earth and I know you are still one in heaven.

To England: Becoming a Man

I'm insanely proud to be Irish. I'm not qualified to write an essay on the Irish Condition and there are many who are, and they have written great books on Irish history and culture. But for me, it's quite simple. In the same way that being an extremely attractive girl can't help but be an advantage in life, *being Irish is a wonderful, natural, head start*. There simply isn't a nation on the planet that it's better to belong to!

I'm forever hearing people talk about "the luck of the Irish". But Is it lucky to have lost half our population to potato blight and famine? Is it lucky to have lived in the shadow of British oppression? And Is it lucky to be born on an island where half the Atlantic Ocean drops on you most days?

Well, I believe the Irish *are* lucky, and for one simple reason – we make our own luck. Your typical Irishman is optimistic, he loves life and the people in it, has inborn charm, and will grin, smile or laugh at almost everything that life throws at him.

The Irish are a suppressed race. We're fighters by necessity, persistent. At the lowest points in my life, I've looked in the mirror and thought "being Irish is all I have left. If I wasn't Irish, I would have given up. But I am, and I haven't!

* * *

Daddy went back to England soon after Mammy's funeral and Maureen went with him. I came in from work one day soon after, and another shock; Doney had gone. Where? To England. He came in from work at 5pm and had emigrated by 6pm. He didn't have much to pack, but surely he had to go in the Guinness Book of Records as fastest emigrator in the world.

Doney disappearing emphasised the hole in our family that had been made by Mammy's death. With Mammy alive, the family would have sat around the table together, and we would have been told that Doney was going to England. But with Mammy gone, we lost our centre.

It was a real blow to lose Doney, I suddenly felt really alone. I wasn't even sure whether or not to believe them. My world had been emptied so many times - how deep must my well have been? Either it was bottomless, or the Good Lord must have kept filling my world back up with energy. Or maybe Mammy was still by my side. I was very sad. Granny, little James and Mammy gone to heaven, and Daddy, Maureen and Doney gone to England.

Then Daddy came back for the rest of us. Benny and Vincie were left to sort the house and furniture. We didn't have a lot, but Daddy advised us to bring as much meat and poultry as we could carry, as rationing was still in force in 1952. The hardest job I had was to twist and crack the necks of all our hens and ducks; after just three or four I felt sick. I asked Pat to hold them over the chopping block and I used the hatchet to chop their heads off. One of the hens' bodies ran off like Roadrunner, while Pat was still holding his head, as if following a pre-planned escape strategy, straight into the hedge. And it simply disappeared – Pat and I scrabbled around for ten minutes but couldn't find it, so we went back to finishing the job in hand. A neighbour's dog or a bunch of crows will have had a great feast on that!

The trip across the Irish Sea was horrendous. The ship, the *Princess Maud,* was built in Cork, and it certainly bounced up and down like one, lacking refinements like stabilisers. Apparently it had been a troop carrier in the Normandy landings in 1944, and was not built for comfort! On the journey from Dun Laoghaire to Holyhead, which should have taken less than two hours, we were swept three hours off course by high winds and waves – people were saying we were going to end up in Normandy, or even in America. Although this was not uncommon for the Princess Maud, it wasn't funny – I had a job to go to in England!

As we sat on benches on the deck, I hung onto the big sack of dead birds for dear life, as if we would starve in England if I let it slip overboard. There were pigs, sheep and geese everywhere – we weren't the only ones to bring our dinner with us, but at least we'd killed ours before setting off! Almost everyone, including me, was sick, all over the place. I was pleased to see big waves come over the boat; one minute there was puke everywhere, seconds later a wet shiny floor. Watching this transformation helped to pass the time.

The train trip from Holyhead wasn't much better. No puke, but no seats either, and cramped! I stood for

LITTLE FECKER!

most of the journey with my face pressed into the armpit of a big old fella, the birds on the floor between my legs. At one point the train broke down and had to reverse all the way back to Crewe. After the ferry crossing it seemed like an eternity, but we eventually got to Stanley Road, Nuneaton. I still had the big sack of ducks and chickens on my back, and felt I had won my first battle. My time in England was going to go well!

Daddy had made some good friends in Nuneaton, and we were made very welcome by his landlord and landlady, Mr and Mrs Goodyear. A completely new life. Doney and I stayed with Daddy, and Rose and Bernie were nearby. Although Maureen was undoubtedly an attractive young woman, I was shocked to find that she had already married, and she and Rita lived with Desi, Maureen's husband. They seemed to have settled in well. Benny and Vincie were still in Ireland, so the young Kellys were spread far and wide, a far cry from ten in one house. But we were happy, we still had one another.

When Daddy married Mr & Mrs Goodyear's daughter, Joan, most of us moved into a four-bedroomed house in the Stockingford part of Nuneaton. Over the next thirteen years Daddy and Joan had three children together, Susan, Paul and Lynne, the Kelly family was still growing!

Benny and Vincie eventually came over, though it was a few days after they were due that they turned up at the Goodyear house in Stanley Road, Nuneaton, as they'd been directed by a helpful fellow traveller to

Stanley Road in Coventry, eleven miles away. We were quite concerned, but knew they would turn up eventually.

Although I should have gone to school, I didn't bother - I was working at Sterling Metals from day one. I had to earn money to pay for my digs. Father Cox from Our Lady of the Angels begged me to go to school for six months. He even came to the Sterling to see me. I told him if he could give me more than £2 10 shillings a week I would gladly go to school! He told me I was being ridiculous. When I told him – truthfully – that I had been working full time for the last two and a half years in Ireland, he gave up.

Sterling Metals, the pits...

I never held anything against Daddy. He was the head of the family and I loved him and respected him unconditionally. When I came to England I was lucky that I didn't have to live far from him, and now at the Sterling I would be working at the same factory. I used to tell anyone who criticised Daddy, "Don't forget, thousands of Irishmen never went back for their families after the war."

In the years ahead I would get itchy feet and work away from home, but I never lost touch with Daddy. Although all of us were working hard and for long hours, whenever and wherever there was work to be had, if I was in Nuneaton on a weekend, Benny, Vincie and Pat would come over from Coventry, and Doney and I would take Daddy to join them at the bingo hall or the Co-op Club. Daddy loved the bingo

LITTLE FECKER!

and win or lose he would laugh and smile for the whole session. It was great to be there with him and my brothers.

But for now I was at home. Sterling Metals was a major employer in Nuneaton, employing between six and seven thousand at any one time. I worked in No.2 Plant on the machines moulding, it was noisy and dusty - the smell of sulphur choked you. Piecework, I certainly earned my £2 10 shillings!

The journey to and from work was on an old Monty Moreton bus. It was a real experience getting on that bus at 6.45 in the morning. With the prospect of an entire day spent breathing shit, the journey was the worst kind of preparation - the bus was always packed solid, and everyone had a fag on except me. I've never ever smoked, in fact after watching the fags kill Granny and Mammy, not one of the nine surviving Kelly kids were ever smokers.

I wish any smoker today could experience that bus journey just once - you have never seen or heard coughing and spluttering like it. Everyone spitting out what they had inhaled the day before in the foundry, but adding to it, by choice, with cigarettes! I felt like I was a million miles from the fresh fields of County Dublin. As someone who likes the pub and the betting shop, I danced a jig when smoking in public places was banned in 2007!

I also worked in the core shop, which led to my first encounter with sex. My job involved fetching a fine powder, like chalk, from the powder room. On my very first day I got cornered in there by four women, who were obviously intent on giving me an 'initiation'. They held me down, whipped my trousers down to my knees and with big handfuls of powder they each had a rub of my Irish shillelagh. They were all having a good laugh, and thinking back there was nothing serious or threatening about it. Being a very shy lad I was very embarrassed at the time.

But this was nothing compared to my next encounter with a female co-worker. One day a week or two later, I was sitting at the bench, eating lunch and having a cup of tea. I felt a tug on my baggy trousers, then got this warm feeling around my shillelagh. As I went to push myself away from the bench so I could look underneath, a female voice said "Don't look down! Relax, and eat your lunch." Without going into detail, it was the best sausage sandwich I ever had, although I did bite my tongue a couple of times!

Fun and games aside, six months later, with my chest and lungs feeling like they were covered in layers of foundry shit and sulphur, I jacked the job in. The old foundry boss begged me to stay, saying I was a good worker, one of the best, and if I stayed I could be one of the best-paid in the country within three years. But I wasn't listening, and to this day I'm glad I didn't. Daddy did stay at the foundry, and it killed him.

Monday morning I was standing alongside one of the finest, most respected men in Nuneaton. Builder Fred Pallet was a big man: 6′ 4″ and built like a brick shit house. In his big black Crombie coat and Quaker-style hat, he interviewed me in his works yard. I told him

LITTLE FECKER!

I'd left the Sterling because of the dusty conditions, and he gave me the start without hesitation.

My first job was a big house on Lutterworth Road, the most sought-after address in Nuneaton. Ironically, I was to buy a house on that road some 27 years later!

Pallets was a good firm to work for, Mr Pallet looked after his men very well. I had a great craic with the lads. In our gang was a lad called Dagwood Hadley; he and his singing partner, Norman 'the Thrush' Hussey, were the kings of the comedy in Nuneaton. When you worked with 'Dags' your ribs would ache, not from carrying the hod but from laughing.

Sadly Dags died in 2003, and as far as I know he and Norman were never honoured for their selfless and wonderful work; they did thousands of gigs for charities, hospices and homes for senior citizens, providing 40 years of free entertainment.

Pallets built half of Nuneaton's huge council housing estate, Camp Hill, with brick houses, while Wimpey built the other half, concrete houses. In the 1970's Pallets went on to build a more expensive estate in the town, St. Nicholas Park, under the reins of Fred's son, Harvey Pallet, and it's nice to see a road there named after the Pallet family.

Despite the tough conditions and dust I had experienced at the Sterling, I decided to try a stint down the mines. I was trained at Daw Mill and went down Arley Pit. I thought the camaraderie at the Sterling had been good, but down the mines it was even stronger. I learned that the more dangerous the job, the closer the teamwork – a lesson emphasised even further when I later joined the army.

I've never been shy of hard work, but the conditions were tough. Each part of the mine had a nickname, and I ended up at 'Butts Corner', a transmission point for the thousands of tons of coal that came out of the Arley Pit every week, uncoupling the full wagons coming back from the coalface. A dangerous job, especially if you put your head between two wagons while coupling up, which was sometimes unavoidable. A 'head sandwich' did hurt but I was lucky – on one occasion I pulled my head out of my safety helmet one second before it was crushed.

All in all, the pit was a good experience, to see and take part in how life was lived miles under the ground. Many men were injured, in fact many were killed getting the black stuff out of the ground so we could have the comfort of the open fire.

On the Road

After nine months down the pit, my feet were as itchy as a squirrel with pepper on his arse. I felt I had to do something with my life. One Sunday, I was having a lunchtime pint with Vincie and a pal called Sean Quinn. It was coming into winter, and where there was work above ground, the hours were being reduced due to the shorter days.

I'd heard that a Nottingham company called North Midland Construction couldn't get enough men, especially Irish men. The Paddies were good at manual labour, and when it came to digging, it was said we could throw the muck further than anyone, even the Poles. I suggested to the lads that if we went to Nottingham, we could sign up as a small gang or join a larger one. And if we packed our bags now, and got to Nottingham before five o'clock, we would be able to start work tomorrow.

We finished our pints, had one more for luck, and raced home to pack a bag. Then we were off, as easy as that. Daddy and Joan were out at church, so we left them a note.

The three of us jumped on a Midland Red bus and headed for Nottingham via Leicester. The one-way fare cost us our last few shillings – of course, we shouldn't have had that last pint! I made a phone call to a mate who worked for North Midland; he spoke to someone in the office and told me that if we got work, the company would sub us a few quid and fix us up with digs when we got there.

Unfortunately we missed the Nottingham bus, and found ourselves on the Great North Road with no transport, no digs and no money. We tried to hitch a lift with no luck, so walked for several miles until we came to a village. We enquired at the church, and the vicar advised us to carry on hitching. He gave us an address in Nottingham for a place called the Spikes. Sean wasn't happy, he had experience of the Spikes, they were poor houses full of down and outs, dossers. It cost a shilling to stop overnight and your belongings were locked up. You also had to work the next day for several hours to pay for your stay and a bit of porridge.

We decided to sleep in the field opposite the church. I wasn't very happy because I felt it was me who had let the lads down. Anyway, we unpacked our heavy coats and shirts to use as blankets, and used the cases for pillows. It has got to be one of the worst nights I'd ever spent. The church bell would *ding-dong* on the quarter, *ding-dong, ding-dong* on the half hour, and all hell would let loose on the hour! And it seemed that every time we did manage to doze off, we were immediately woken by the squealing of rats! I thought I had got away from them a long time ago.

Rats are very clever; the high-pitched squealing was their way of finding out whether we were alive. If you are lying in a field and are not disturbed by their squealing, then they will investigate further, they will come closer.

Back in Ireland, we had a very sad experience one night. One of our puppies was barking, and rats were squealing. But it was dark, pitch black, and we were all too afraid to go round the back of the shed. The next morning we found the little puppy dead. It had got trapped in a gap between the planks in the shed, the rats knew the pup was helpless so they gouged out its throat and chest. We were very upset.

So, in Leicester, we threw a couple of boots at the hedge to let the rats know we weren't easy meat. But before we could doze off again, it was time to get up. We packed our gear and set off on foot – between us we had just fourpence. Having lugged our heavy cases so far, we couldn't drag them around as we searched for work and breakfast, so we went to Leicester train station. The left luggage lockers at station cost twopence each, so we squeezed our three big bags into two lockers.

We were starving and couldn't buy breakfast. We didn't know how to beg, the only asset we had that I could see was Sean's sports jacket, possibly fifty quid's worth. The last thing Sean wanted to do was pawn his lovely coat. I convinced him we would be working soon, so he could come and buy it back. He gave in, and we went into a pawn shop. I hated pawn shops – the people who own and run them are trained to make you feel like a piece of shite. The bloke behind the counter looked like another rat – we could see that he was going to say the coat was worth nothing before Sean even took it off.

He kept saying, I'll give you thirty shillings", and he wouldn't budge. That's £1.50.

"You're a shite, that'll barely buy three breakfasts!" I said. A stand-off – he was protected by a sturdy iron grid, but could see I was losing my temper, and the grid wouldn't have stopped me. Balling my fists and gritting my teeth, I could see the red mist.

"OK, I'll give you fifty shillings." £2.50. Better.

It was 10am, into the café we went, like hungry dogs. We ordered three full breakfasts, hoping for generous portions, breakfasts fit for hardworking men. But we were out of luck. A shrivelled bacon rasher, one egg, one sausage and a spoonful of runny tomatoes, two thin slices of bread. It was completely out of character for me, but I sensed that this might be our only meal of the day. I went into the kitchen, and begged the woman for some more bread.

"Just any old bits on the heel of the loaf will do, love" I said, with my best charming smile. Fair play to her, she came out with a whole loaf of bread and a saucepan of hot tomatoes.

"There you are," she said, "get that down you". An angel. She even gave us an address where we might pick up some work.

She told us that a company called Monk Construction was doing a lot of work in the area, and that a lot of their workers stayed in the Derwent Pub. We headed straight there. The Derwent was now a guesthouse with about thirty lodgers. Though the bar counter was still intact, the bar was a dining room. Shame.

When we arrived, the obvious thing to do was to tell the landlady we were workers with Monk. It worked well; we had a roof over our head and a belly full of food. We chatted up the lads to try and get work, and prospects seemed promising, but when we got to speak to the gaffers it turned out that they weren't setting on. So we had no option but to stay out of the digs all day, and come in at the same time as the rest of the gang in the evening so we could get dinner. Our plan was to scarper the next morning after a good breakfast, but when we saw the lads queuing for big packs of sandwiches for lunch, we joined the queue, grabbed the food and headed for the park. We did look for work at the council and with various firms of small builders, but with no luck.

After three days the landlady was getting suspicious; she noticed how clean we were when we came in from work; most of the lads were covered in muck. Tomorrow, Thursday, would be payday, for those in work at least. The landlady said she wanted her money tomorrow or else, and the lads told us that when she caught cheats she always called the police.

We planned our escape. Next morning, we had the cheek to have breakfast, then go back upstairs to get our gear together. We put on as many clothes as we could, I had four shirts, two pairs of trousers and two coats on, I could hardly move. Downstairs we got in the queue for sandwiches.

Leaving behind anything that we couldn't wear, a load of gear, we took sandwiches and walked out. Sean had won a few quid in a game of cards (though not enough to rescue his best coat from the pawn shop), and gave me the bus fare back to Nuneaton while he and Vincie headed for the Great North Road. They got arrested and were bound over after promising to pay back the landlady.

I felt guilty – I'd gotten off lightly and left my brother to face the music. My only real loss from the affair was that I had forgotten my harmonica. I left it under my pillow in the Derwent, and though it served me right, I was quite sick about it. It was a good one I'd bought while I was working at the Sterling – it would set you back about £200 today.

1955 – enjoying a well-earned pint with Doney

After that, Vincie, Doney and I drifted from job to job, working up and down the country for companies like McAlpine. We did work for North Midland later, before returning to Nuneaton. I went to work for a local builder called Wincott, they asked me to work nights for a month, painting steelwork and pipework. The money was good with the night allowance so I took it. But I ended up in the fecking Sterling Metals, with me paint brush, back in the shit again.

LITTLE FECKER!

After several weeks of nights, I started to get quite severe stomach-ache. I rarely went to the doctor, but the pain was so terrible that I was forced to visit the family GP, Doctor McKeown. He asked where I was working, what I was eating, all routine stuff. When I told him I had carried on eating my usual three full meals during the day, as well as the meals provided in the Sterling's canteen during the night shift, the doctor gave me a quizzical look and told me to drop my trousers. He asked me to bend over, and walked round me in a circle without so much as touching me.

"I see the problem, Mr Kelly," he said, in a grave tone.
"You do?" I wondered what he could have seen.
"Yes. You only have one arsehole."

He was joking, of course, but it wasn't funny. Not funny at all. He sent me straight to hospital. I never really thought I had any enemies, but I was about to have something similar – an enema. I should have guessed what was coming when the nurse told me where the toilet was before she pulled my underpants down. A once-in-a-lifetime experience, I hope!

The enema was cleansing in more ways than one. I made a decision: no more Sterling, no more coalmines, no more painting. I could smell tarmac again, the feet were itching.

I found out where Vincie was working and headed east to Godmanchester, Cambridgeshire. We were a few miles from the Great North Road, working for the Northwest Construction Company. We were contracted to lay cable ducts, in trenches two foot wide and two foot six deep. First we had to dig the long trenches, then manhandle the large, heavy four-way and six-way glazed pot ducts. But that was no problem - we were as strong as silverback gorillas. Everything was a challenge and we enjoyed every minute. No responsibility whatsoever.

After a few months on the cable ducts, Vincie and I teamed up with Sean again and we were on our travels. Doney joined us as we finally landed up in Nottingham. Well, little had changed - we were skint again, the dogs and the horses we picked weren't running fast enough.

Of course, we had to get out for a pint. There's nothing more boring than a small bedroom in a dingy guest house, and when you've got no money for beer the call of the pub is even greater. So the four of us were standing outside a pub on Mansfield Road Nottingham, apparently the last on the route to Gallows Hill, where condemned prisoners were allowed a last drink, paid for by the landlord, before meeting their maker.

It sounded just the job to us, but when we got there we found we were expected to pay for our drinks! The landlord wasn't keen on us hanging around - with no money for drink, all we were likely to do was cause trouble, and he didn't seem to fancy having to handle four strapping Paddies.

But we needed to chat to some people in the bar, because we had to get someone to give us an address for new digs. Sean set out to find a fellow countryman

LITTLE FECKER!

with a kind face, and fortunately Irishmen are not too hard to spot. Sean found one and asked to borrow sevenpence each for a half of mild, but came back with a fiver in his hand, so it was four pints each, and plenty of change for more! Word got around that we were looking for digs, as we had a job to start the next morning. Someone made a phone call and we were fixed up for the night.

I've travelled quite a bit, but in all my travels I have never seen anything quite like the place we ended up in that night. As we made our way up to rooms on the 3rd floor, the stairs were lined on both sides with milk bottles full of liquid, and from the pungent smell it was clear that the liquid was piss. Every step had at least four bottles with green plastic tops, full to the brim, and a narrow path up the middle. The higher we went, the more bottles there were, till we were taking the stairs four at a time just to find gaps for our feet. Believe me, a field full of rats held more appeal.

I found a toilet – it was disgusting. Someone told me there was a second in the building – it was worse. Two toilets in the whole place, and you would have needed to take out a life policy before daring to sit on either. The house must have had fifty lodgers - I couldn't understand how once clean men could live in conditions like this. I didn't know how a landlord or landlady could let a place get into such a state. . Needless to say we left before breakfast.

Next stop was a two month contract at Weedon, on the A5. The digs weren't too bad, seven beds in a big first floor room. The house, a former police station, was by a canal, so I was back with my old friends – the rats. I never saw them, but as soon as we got into bed, they were flying and squealing up and down the void between the downstairs ceiling and our floor. You have never heard such a din. We'd bang the floor with our heavy boots to get a bit of peace, and the squeal of rats would be joined by a roar from downstairs.

"Pack in fecking banging, or there'll be trouble!" came the cry from below. But one of our room-mates, an Aberdonian called Jock, decided to carry on banging. Suddenly the door burst open, bodies poured in and a fight broke out. I couldn't tell in the melee how many men had come in to attack us, and there was so much blood flying about that nobody had any idea who won the fight, but eventually things quietened down, as they do. When the dust settled, two of the beds were legless, one of them mine. So two of us were on the floor, just a thin mattress and a plank between us and our noisy rat friends. I think they were playing five-a-side. A bit close for comfort.

A week later the place was suddenly closed down, it could have been the health inspectors after the rats. Vincie and I found digs in Upper Heyford. The landlady had never had lodgers before, so she couldn't do enough for us. They had a very pretty daughter, about my age, and Vincie and I were both hoping she might be as amenable as her mother, but she wasn't interested in us. The man of the house was the eight year-old son - a right little sod – and there was a Jack Russell dog and a big fat cat.

LITTLE FECKER!

One evening after dinner, Vincie, the daughter and I were sitting in the lounge, listening to the radio. The son was sitting on the floor. The dog was panting like mad and yapping, and I noticed the lad was playing with its dick. The cat, in front of the fire, was minding its own business. Suddenly, in what must have been a well-practiced manoeuvre, the lad grabbed the cat with one hand, and stuck the Jack Russell on top of it with the other. The dog started pumping like its life depended on it, the cat nearly shot through the roof. While the young fellow got a wallop from his mother, the daughter winked, grinned and left.

* * *

Though I'd had many scrapes with death back home in Ireland, I hadn't had a near-death experience since arriving in England. When I was asked to work two weeks on nights, looking after a set of temporary traffic lights, I couldn't see how it might be more dangerous than a foundry or the mines.

My job was to make sure there was fuel in the generator and that the bulbs in the traffic lights were working. The first week went well; I was used to hard manual graft and this was just an exercise in staying awake for an hour at a time on a hard chair in a six-foot square hut. Once an hour I'd have to nip out to check the lights just outside the shed, then walk half a mile up the road in the freezing cold to check the other set. Yes, no problem, walk half a mile back.

Lighting in the hut was provided by paraffin lamps. These old things threw out more heat than light, and I was so cold and tired that I decided to light all three lamps to keep warm. That's better… cosy…

"Breathe in! Now out!" I was dreaming. Someone was shouting at me. I was lying by the road outside the shed, in the headlamp beam and blue flashing lights of an ambulance. My stomach felt twisted, my head was thumping. No dream. The man shouting was a paramedic. I had fallen asleep, the lamps had leaked deadly carbon fumes, and there was no oxygen in the hut.

Two things saved my life that night. First, the generator powering the traffic lights ran out of fuel, so they stopped working. Second, a trucker, who could so easily have just gone on his way, saw the light in my hut and decided to investigate. He found me unconscious in the hut, and it took him ten minutes to bring me round. If the light had not broken down, he would have had no reason to stop. But he did stop, and he saved my life. I never got to thank him - he was a saint.

The ambulance men put me on oxygen for half an hour, then took me back to my digs. They told me that if the generator hadn't run out of fuel I would be a dead man. I felt blessed, and not for the first time!

The working life was much like the thrashing days back in Ireland, except I was using a shovel instead of a fork and there weren't so many rats around - except in the digs. The contract finished and our gang of about ten split up and went to different sites.

LITTLE FECKER!

Vincie and I got work with Beechams Concrete, who built and maintained big buildings. We were given the address for our first job. Feck me, we landed up at the Sterling Metals Foundry, again! Was I ever going to get away from the place?

Beechams had the contract to build the new Number One foundry, and Vincie and I were set on to work on the footings. It was tough work, digging solid sandstone, but at least we were in the fresh air, and we could breathe. Not like our Daddy who was still in there, breathing shite, smoking twenty fags a day and coughing more than he talked. I wondered why he spent money on fags, when he couldn't see his hand in front of his face for the smoke he spent ten hours a day in.

Daddy was a tough man, six feet tall and hard as nails. He didn't get into many fights but one of the lads at the Sterling told me they'd seen him in a fight in the old Queen's Head in Nuneaton. Apparently he was having a drink at a table with a lady friend, and a Polish bloke made a comment about the lady.

The man was standing over the two of them. As Daddy got up, he launched a right hook which hit the Pole square in the jaw and floored him. What Daddy hadn't seen was that there were two more Polish blokes standing at the bar. They dived on Daddy and the fight proper started. The first Pole got up and dived in too, and the chap telling me the story said the fight went on for fifteen or twenty minutes. Daddy, cheered on by everyone in the busy pub, but apparently helped by no-one, won 3-0.

Ironically, Beechams employed mostly Polish people. Just like the Paddies, they never knew when to stop working. So here we were, me and Vincie, working alongside a big crew of Polish men. I have great respect for the Polish, and as well as building a foundry I was building lifelong friendships.

As well as a mean right hand, Daddy had a wicked sense of humour. There's no doubt that I got my sense of mischief from him. Christmas with him in Nuneaton was every bit as special as in the old days in Kilbride. One year we went for a few pints on Christmas Eve, and when I say a few I mean a fair few – we rolled rather than walked out of the Cock and Bear pub. I tuned right to walk home, but Daddy turned left. "Joan asked me to get a turkey off the market – the biggest one they have."

So Daddy brought home a big bird, we had a few more drinks and all went to bed. At about 6.30am on Christmas morning we were all woken by Joan. She was screaming. And Joan could scream.

"Danny! Danny! Daniel!"

The whole house stirred, we all sort of fell into the kitchen to see what was wrong. I half expected to see that Joan had clobbered a burglar with a big frying pan.

"Daniel! This turkey! It's got a big yellow beak!"

Daddy grinned, put his arm round Joan, probably so she couldn't swing a frying pan, and gently told her that the turkey… was a goose. Now whether he had brought home a goose accidentally or for the sheer craic, we never found out. Daddy just grinned, with a big Irish twinkle in his eye. We roared.

Fighting and Gambling

I was once walking in Nuneaton with Doney, and we came across two blokes fighting outside a pub. I knew both men, and there was no-one else around, so Doney and I tried to stop the fight. Instead we managed to set in place a chain reaction: everyone poured out onto the street, to see me and Doney apparently fighting with two of the pub's regulars. So what started as a peace-making mission ended up with me and Doney being attacked by about seventeen blokes - including the two who had been fighting each other! I have been in many fights over the years, and many of these started because I had been trying to make the peace.

But breaking up fights is in the Kelly blood. Vincie was another peacemaker. We were both sharp and aware of potentially dangerous situations, but it always amazed me how many blokes we came up against were the sort who would hit their own grandmother.

Vincie and I often won these fights. Benny too would often wade in, but more because he enjoyed the sport than to stop anyone else getting hurt. If big Benny was with us we almost certainly won – he was unstoppable. But after the event I often felt that it would have been better to lose. You would win a fight but gain a whole load of new enemies, not only the men you hit (who would as often as not forgive you, shake hands and have a pint with you), but their friends, their girlfriends, their families. You would be labelled, and none of these would forget what you'd done. You would be their enemy for life – and they would have no interest in the circumstances, the reasons why there was a fight in the first place.

I worry about this when I look at street fighting today. It's a different game. The youth of today bear grudges and many carry weapons. If Benny ever caught anyone with a knife he'd break their arm – I saw him do it twice. I would certainly not get involved as a peacemaker today (even though I know, at 77, I'm still capable) for fear of the recriminations.

One exception to wishing I had lost, was one night in Preston. I was with Vincie and about seven other lads, we were in a pub where there was music and dancing. Over the course of the evening we found ourselves sitting with a bunch of girls, and Vincie and I were buying these two girls their drinks – bottles of Guinness and lime, an expensive drink.

At about ten o'clock the music stopped, and all of a sudden a bunch of lads appeared from the other bar. Two of them unceremoniously pushed their way onto our table, between me, Vincie and the girls. Vincie looked at me – he could see I wasn't going to be liking this!

"What's the craic?" I asked. The girls blushed. "These are our boyfriends."

LITTLE FECKER!

Well, feck me. I wasn't expecting to get me leg over or anything, but I felt it was a bit of a con trick, for these lads to leave us to buy their girls' drinks all night. But Vincie gave me the look that said "Leave it, Ned." And I did. Well, I did… until we got to the chip shop. There was a long queue, and at the front, these same two lads were buying chips for the girls.

"Hey, I'll have a fish and chips, thanks!" I shouted.
"What are you on about?" one of the lads smirked.
"Well, I've been buying your girl's drinks all night – in fact, we'll have two *large* fish and chips, and a couple of quid! That's fair, that should square us!"

The lad was having none of it. He sneered and turned back to the counter. I was fuming! Again Vincie nudged me to leave it. And I probably would have, but to get out of the shop the lad had to pass me in the queue, and as he did, he smirked again. Bad idea.

My fist shot up, under his two trays of fish, chips and mushy peas. We both looked up as the peas hit the ceiling, in an arty splat.

I rarely, if ever, start a fight, I'm always proud not to have thrown the first punch, but on this one occasion I felt justified. And as the lad looked down again, my other fist caught him under the chin.

There was, of course, quite a melee outside the chip shop – two bunches of eight lads giving it everything for five minutes until the girls' screaming eventually made us all stop. No-one was badly hurt – that was never the aim – and we all went home.

The answer, of course, is to avoid fights; I always tried to do that, and still do today. For example, even at my age I still prefer to drink in pubs with small bars – limited space means less room for fighting. If I'm forced to drink in a large saloon, I take a position facing the main doors and with my back to the wall. It's not that I'm looking for trouble, and I'm certainly not afraid of it, but old habits die hard!

So I hope you'll appreciate by now that yes, I'm a fighter, but I pick my fights. Usually I've fought to help someone else. And when it comes to fighting an enemy I can see, I usually come off best.

I love amateur boxing. Tuesday and Thursday I'd find a gym somewhere and go and train. I loved it, a lovely skill. I rate it very highly; if you can get kids off the street and give them confidence, discipline and something to do, they're less likely to get into trouble. Dave Thompson used to tell them "don't come here, learn how to fight and take it into the streets, if you see a fight, stand back and try to stop it. Professional boxer has lethal weapons – don't use them in the street".

Years later, I joined the committee at the Bulkington Sports & Social Amateur Boxing Club. I built a ring for them, and I once entered a carnival float with boxers boxing in a ring. It was a highly rated club, founded by former Scottish ABA light-middle-weight champion Dave Thompson, my good friend Bob Darlaston and Stewart Tidman, and it's now one of the top amateur boxing clubs in the country.

LITTLE FECKER!

With the CIP-sponsored boxers at Bulkington BC

Another pastime of mine is gambling. Always within my means, and for fun, but I do like a flutter. I guess it's in the blood. Doney did a bit but Vincie, Pat and I always gambled, every day as far back as I can remember. In the old days the lads at work used to play poker every Thursday, as soon as we collected our wages at 3pm. One particular day the foreman came in at 6.30pm and said that he had clocked us all out at 4pm. We thanked him and continued playing... until breakfast next morning. I remember it well because I won three weeks' wages.

Gambling for me is all about anticipation. Most gamblers bet on a horse and either watch the race or rush to find the result as soon as possible afterwards. I prefer to bet on horses one day (most days) and not check the results until the next– this has the effect of always giving me something to look forward to.

For the whole time between placing the bet and discovering the result, I am potentially a richer man. I even delay the process of finding the results as much as possible; I avoid fast, modern methods of news retrieval, preferring the traditional newspaper route. The horse racing is in the back of the newspaper, so I always start at the front, delaying until as late as possible the moment when I reach the racing results, and finally find out whether yesterday's bet was a winner. If I haven't won, the disappointment lasts for less than an hour, during which time I'm distracted by the task of choosing my horses for today's bet!

Gambling is a challenge, I study the form and my aim is to get it right and outwit the bookie against the odds. As I hand over my stake, I say "goodbye" to my cash, and "see you tomorrow!" to the bookie.

I've always liked the horses but rarely go to race meetings – I don't find that racing and socialising mix well – it's hard to concentrate on one or the other. Gambling on cards or dominos or the like has a sociable element that I really like. I rarely gamble at the pool table - pool is a game I have always loved without having to bet on the outcome of a game.

But fighting and gambling are a single man's hobbies. I was growing up, and starting to think about the opposite sex…

Falling in Love

I would never describe myself as handsome – I'm a sniff under five feet seven, and it's always been my view that a man needs to be tall to be handsome. I trained hard as a boxer in my youth, and have always had a decent chest and solid pair of shoulders, and I suppose as I filled out in my twenties and thirties I maybe became more attractive.

Making an effort in the late 50's

I've always had a good head of hair, and still do. It was mousy brown when I was young (my nickname was "mousy" for many years), then it turned dark in my late twenties. I didn't start to go grey until I was 50. Daddy had amazing thick white hair, mine's more silver with dark bits, but I'm not complaining!

My voice and accent are an asset – my Irish brogue has softened considerably compared with my brothers – I suppose it started with the English influence of the forces, then I've spent so many years mixing with English businessmen, while my brothers have definitely spent more time with other Paddies. I've been asked several times if I'm Canadian, which always surprises me!

But I've always got on with the opposite sex, and I think that's for two reasons. First, I make an effort – just like I make an effort to get on with male friends – and I think ladies appreciate that. And second, I set out to make them laugh – and I guess I turn on the Irish charm a bit sometimes. Chatting up waitresses is always fun, they enjoy the attention, and of course it generally leads to great service. I was in a restaurant once, and the manager came over and whispered to me: "Sorry about the delay with your food – I think your waitress has gone to adjust her knickers!"

In 1955, I got work at the fairground in Nuneaton as a "Guess Your Weight" man, employing a trick of the horse-racing trade I had learned from Charlie Rogers. Way back when I had hopes of becoming a jockey, Rogers had gauged my weight, and even guessed - correctly - that I would gain weight, simply by grabbing my wrist, ankle and upper arm.

So I practiced a bit on family and friends, then at the fairground I would do the same. But I would disguise what I was doing by pretending I was trying to lift people off the ground. I would make quite a fuss and palaver of sizing up my 'victim', getting them to undo their coat before walking around them, stepping back a few paces, squinting my eyes and sucking in a breath, before making comedic attempts to pick them up by their wrists or ankles or both (if they were small or pretty or both I might actually pick them up).

LITTLE FECKER!

My antics ensured a large crowd, and when I correctly guessed the weight within a pound or two almost every time, they'd be queuing for their turn. Before long there would be meatheads who were going to lie about their weight whatever I said, but I soon got around that, by borrowing a big set of weighing scales from a local butcher. When I say "borrow", a friend who worked for the butcher would sneak them out after the shop closed!

So the fairground was where I got to be a bit of a showman, it was also where I fell in love. Several times, while I was performing my weighing act, I'd see a girl, a tall, slim girl, walk by. This girl was always smiling, and usually laughing, loud and free. I caught her eye once, but she never stopped to watch.

Then, one day, I was sitting with Vincie on the steps of the Cock and Bear pub, at the top of the hill coming out of Nuneaton's town centre towards where I was living in Stockingford (and, perhaps ironically, right next door to Manor Park, the football ground where I was to spend so much of the 1970's and 80's). Vincie and I were just chatting, enjoying the sunshine, when my attention was distracted by two young ladies coming up the hill. One caught my eye – the girl from the fairground, tall, slim, and lovely – she was laughing and her face was brighter than the sun.

I hadn't expected to see this girl again, let alone bump into her so close to home. I jumped up mid-sentence and skipped over to say hello. Her name was Joan Marshall. She was only sixteen, and a bit shy, so she said hello but kept walking. Not to be put off, I launched into a conversation and I kept walking too. Her friend Eunice Dingley didn't get a word in. When we reached the point where Joan and Eunice went their separate ways, I offered to walk Joan home, but she said, "Maybe next time", smiled and was gone.

I hung around the stretch of road where we parted company for the next couple of days, and it paid off – I bumped into Joan again and invited her to see Gone With the Wind at the cinema. She said yes! We got on really well – I think I impressed her with my trick of guzzling a huge bottle of fizzy Tizer pop, scrunching up the metal bottle top, squeezing it into the bottle, and rolling the bottle down the steps of the aisle.

Joan giggled uncontrollably as the poor usher raced down the steps with her torch flashing left and right, trying to spot the origin of the noise – which was really irritating - and catch the culprit. We both struggled to keep a straight face as she came back up the aisle, shining her torch beam full in people's faces.

We held hands as I walked Joan home, and we laughed all the way. I soon learned with Joan that I had a "laughter threshold" of forty five minutes – beyond that I would be in physical pain – face ache – and suffer serious exhaustion! But Joan could laugh forever! On our second cinema trip I put my arm around her, and it was an amazing feeling. And as we reached her front doorstep I gave her a respectful kiss – I had definitely fallen in love!

Working away from home meant that I didn't see as much of Joan as I would have liked. But then a cat was thrown amongst the pigeons that was to keep us apart for a while longer.

National Service

The digs were good in Godmanchester; rooms above the King's Head pub. The food was good too. We were digging a massive brook for Post Office Telephones (now BT), to house an underground transformer. The pay was £25 to £30 a week, and the digs, which included sandwich lunch and a hot evening meal, only cost £5, so we had plenty of money for beer, fun and the betting shop!

Ted St John, the mobile compressor driver on our site, also lived in our digs. He was a very nice man, and let me drive his big lorry. I had no licence then, and driving the truck made me feel really good.

After our meal one evening, we sat having a chat, Ted, Vincie, the landlady's son and myself. The son was at college, and Ted was winding him up about how much I was earning at 18 years old. He pointed out that not only was I better off working than going to college, but also that I was better off keeping out of the army.

Many of my Irish mates thought National Service was a waste of time; the money was so poor they couldn't afford to smoke, and certainly drink was out. How could you go from thirty pints of Guinness a week to being teetotal? Many moved about the country anyway with no fixed address. I had a permanent address in Nuneaton, so I was a resident and they knew where to find me – if they weren't chasing me then I certainly didn't feel it was up to me to go and present myself for National Service.

But of course the landlady's son was bright enough to work out that by travelling around I was avoiding conscription. We were having a great time, but the lad looked like he was sucking a lemon.

I don't think it was a coincidence that three days later an army jeep with three military policemen turned up at my digs. I was given an ultimatum – be arrested or sign a piece of paper that committed me to making arrangements with the Royal Warwickshire Regiment at Budbrooke Barracks to join the next intake.

Doney had already left the gang and returned to work in Coventry, Benny had got him a job, so he was out of the trenches and into a more stable, but still lucrative, trade: pipework engineering. The saddest part of leaving this well-paid work was to be leaving Vincie behind.

Going into the forces was not easy for me. I was in a serious relationship with Joan, and two years was a long time to be away, even if I was to be stationed just twenty miles from Nuneaton, at Budbrooke. What I didn't know as I kissed Joan goodbye was that I was to land up in Cyprus for nearly 16 months.

I turned up at Budbrooke, and it was straight in for a short back and sides. There were six barbers in a row, and a long line of new recruits going through like sheep at a shearing competition. Five of the barbers were using clippers, obviously the easier method, but my guy – who must have been a butcher on Civvy Street – used scissors, and he was as quick as his colleagues!

No messing, there was hair flying all over the place as I said goodbye to my beloved teddy-boy "ducks arse" hairstyle. Well, I'd save a few shillings on Brylcreem at any rate! By the time he'd finished, my hair was brutally short, there was a day's growth left at best. But unlike the neat, shaved heads of the lads in the other chairs, mine was stumpy and uneven – my reflection reminded me of distant Irish days where the hair was cut like this to keep the nits away. I toyed with nipping into the shower and shaving the lot, but was warned that this would be treated as contemptuous. I didn't know what that meant, but it sounded nasty! Fortunately our hair was cut once a week anyway, so I didn't have to put up with it for long, I just had to avoid the old butcher!

I overheard one new recruit offer a barber two shillings and sixpence to "slip" when setting the clippers, so he could just have a little less off. That was fatal. He was the only chap to come out of there with a haircut worse than mine, and then he was sent back by an officer to have his head shaved completely. I spoke to the lad at dinner: "If anyone says you look contemptuous, just ignore them – I don't think it's catching!"

After the hard graft of digging trenches and laying cables, ten weeks of hard training was no trouble, except for the shock at the end of the first week. Pay parade. You had to parade for your money, and you had to look smart. We lined up in rows of four; when your name was called you came to attention, marched across the room and slammed your right foot down, saluted and said "Sir!"

The officer gave me a quid. I looked at him, he looked at me. I raised an eyebrow that said what I was thinking - the performance of getting across the room alone was worth a quid! But his eyes were pure steel. I thought, "grab that quid or you'll get nothing". That's what I call a drop in salary, from £30 to £1 a week.

The next week was worse - I got nothing. I had very quickly taken to the discipline of being neat and tidy, and I was soon o be winning awards or the state of my bed, but in my second week we were penalised because a cat had got into our billet and crapped under a bed. Someone threw the cat out the window. Horses and dogs were also out the window - I couldn't afford gambling, even a game of dominos.

To replace my old hobbies I took up boxing – it was great release and good discipline, I was wiry and small but very strong, and more than a little streetwise when it came to technique. I was quite good.

Training over, nine of us new conscripts were told we were bound for Cyprus. There was big trouble there with the EOKA and they needed extra men. The camp doctor said I could choose to go to Northern Ireland because I had injured my thumb while representing the Army as a boxer. But I wanted to be with the lads I'd trained with, so I accepted the posting.

LITTLE FECKER!

I kissed Joan and said goodbye to the family I loved so much, it felt like I was leaving them properly for the first time. This parting felt so much more definite than leaving to work on the roads for a few weeks or months. I suppose I was starting to grow up.

I have mixed feelings about my time in Cyprus. The troubles had died down a bit, but it was a dangerous place to be. In Famagusta we were confined to barracks or to one of the police stations for most of the time. A full curfew was in operation. We were on internal security, not dissimilar to active service. It would get very boring, nothing at all happening for long stretches of time, then all hell would let loose, a riot in Famagusta or one of the villages.

The worst riot I witnessed was one Sunday in the old city of Famagusta, the Turkish area. The Turks were very upset, because General Harding had left the island to be replaced by Sir Hugh Foot, who made it clear that he felt the Greek Cypriots were not getting a fair deal. The Turks disagreed, and rebelled.

I don't think there is anything more frightening than the sight and sound of over a thousand men, many obviously full of wine, marching towards you, banging on big drums. They were trying to get out of the old city to have a go at the Greek Cypriots, and our job was to prevent this. Seven Turks were shot dead and a lot of soldiers injured on that day.

Apart from incidents like this, we had a lot of time on our hands. We would be on parade at 7am, and keep ourselves busy all morning on various training sessions, guard duties, and protocols. I was getting better at boxing and was invited to represent the Army in local competition against the other forces, so I was spending a lot of my time in training. After six hours' hard graft, at 1pm, we would have lunch. The food was poor, and there was never enough. I was so hungry I could have eaten the sole of my boots.

The afternoons were more of the same. On days when we weren't on duty we were lucky, we could go for a swim in the afternoon. Every chance I got I was out, snorkelling around the rocks. It was another world.

Because I was now overseas, my earnings had increased from £1 to £2 10s (£2.50) per week. But the pay didn't last long. With the meagre food rations, there was often a need to buy extra from the NAAFI, just to stop the rumbling, but it was very expensive. And a pint bottle of Keo beer cost two shillings (10p), so my choice was limited. If I ate, I wouldn't be able to drink on Friday night. I didn't have the expense of taking Joan out - there weren't *any* women to take out; if the single lads wanted a woman, they had to fight over a very popular magazine called the Blighty - the nearest they got to seeing a girl's underwear.

In all the time I was there, we were only allowed to go to the pictures twice. Four of us would go together, and at least one had to be armed with a sten gun.

I came home from Cyprus when the Leicestershire regiment was replaced by the Royal Ulster Rifles. Joan greeted me and we continued our courtship, until I had to report to Crown Hill Barracks in Plymouth.

LITTLE FECKER!

The food there was much better, and the conditions 100% better than living in a tin hut with toilets and washing facilities two hundred yards away.

And oh, the joy of a proper toilet! In Cyprus, toilets were a long plank with a row of holes in. No flushes, no blushes, you just got on with it. A couple of squares of newspaper and the business was done.

You had to watch out for the shit beetles. They were black and yellow, and so big that you could hear them scuttling along on the underside of the plank. And if one got onto your arse, it would cling on with its powerful claw-like legs. A lot of lads were so scared of them (thanks in main to the many exaggerated stories that circulated around the camp) that they would shit standing up. You can imagine this big gang of beetles, waiting and watching all the pink arses every morning, 'Dinner time!'

I always thought that it must have been an odd existence for those beetles. It must have taken them an age to crawl from the bottom of the shit hole, which was about twenty feet deep, to the plank. It was a long way to come for a quick sniff, I always felt it was like a treat for them, a weekend away. One sure thing, you didn't sit there reading the paper!

Some of the lads had trouble with acclimatisation. There was often trouble between groups of forces lads, or between forces lads and locals, in the pubs on Union Street. There were the MATLO'S, the Americans, and various military regiments.

Plymouth was a garrison town. One of our lads had spent three years in the Sudan without a single holiday. On leaving the Sudan, he was convinced he was on his way home, but they dumped him in Cyprus for another year. Many men in Plymouth had suffered similarly - can you imagine a young, fit soldier, after four years without a single day of female company, arriving in Plymouth, with its fleshpot pubs and clubs? After six pints they went mad.

I wasn't to stay in Plymouth for long. I was drafted, with three of my mates, to Holywell Bay, a small village south of Newquay in Cornwall. It was summer, and we were looking after an officers' mess. This was great, we had free rein to eat all the food and drink all the wine we could get down us. To offset the effects of excessive eating and drinking, we volunteered to do lifeguard duty, as the currents there were very dangerous. There was plenty of beer and life was better than in Cyprus.

For the first time I thought the army wasn't too bad after all, and I was glad I had joined up.

I finished my two years with a civil defence course in Cumbernauld, then it was back to Civvy Street. I wondered where Vincie was.

I moved back in with Daddy and Joan. Pat and Bernie were also living there. Rita, who had grown up to be a beautiful, glamorous young lady, lived nearby, working for Finn's Shoes and winning major beauty competitions. I was pleased to learn that Vincie was working in Bulkington and living with Maureen, just five miles down the road. Pat was working for a sheet metal company, and Benny lived in Coventry.

So we had the family back together. I think Benny could tell that my feet were itching again - after two years in the Army, shackled by rules, forced to stay in one place with no control over my life, I could smell the tarmac of the Great North Road. But Benny, bless his soul, got me a job working with him and Doney at Carrier's Engineering. This was a major turning point for me: the job at Carrier's distracted me from leaving the nest again, as I trained to be a pipefitter-welder and laid foundations that would set me up in business for the next thirty five years.

We worked a lot of overtime; a normal week was 80 hours, with "ghosters" on top of that. But it wasn't easy settling back into work, a life of routine. My love for Joan persuaded me. We were engaged now, how could we get married if I was away digging trenches? It was time for me to bury my walking boots and pick up the welding torch.

After Carrier's I worked for Daly's, seven days a week to save up to get married. I was fabricating pipework for a boiler house in Foxford School when a man named Bert Timmins offered me a job. He was a foreman for Sulzer Brothers, a Swiss company. I took the job and the money was good, but I ended up travelling again as they had contracts all over the country. Although the first move was only to Wolverhampton, it was too far for my battered old Vauxhall Velox, which couldn't stand the pace, so I got digs.

My last two contracts as an employee sum up why I decided to set up on my own.

I won a contract to remove a chemical plant from a Courtaulds factory in Liverpool and rebuild it at a site in Preston. Preparation for a job like this was vital, but I was given no paperwork, no drawings and no guidance. The plant was entirely fabricated in six-inch and four-inch pipework, all lagged and covered in wire mesh with boxed flanges, and there were six large chemical vessels holding three thousand gallons each. Some were lead lined - these had to be shuttered out with wood housings.

I set the lads to work, instructing them to remove every bolt except two in each set, while I sat in our hut working out my plan. Every joint and every piece of pipe had to be numbered and tagged. I hired a photographer to take dozens of pictures from every angle before the dismantling started, including all the steel work housing. I had to hire cranes, low loaders, carpenters and sign makers. Two weeks after we started, the bosses of the company came to Aintree to see how we were getting on. They were surprised to find no one on site – we had gone, and so had the plant. It was being re-erected in Preston.

In nine months I won tens of thousands of pounds of new work on that site, but received no reward or even appreciation form the company. The lads would tell me every day; "You should start up on your own".

My final contract was at a chemical plant outside Wellingborough, huge cooling towers, with twelve-

LITTLE FECKER!

inch pipework, a beauty. Half way through the contract, the chief engineer of the client company called me into his office to discuss how the job was going. We both knew we were running behind schedule. I explained that my boss was trying to get a couple of extra welders to speed things up.

He looked me in the eye and said, "Can you get your men to unload all the veg from under the seats of your mini-bus?" This company owned a vegetable farm and you would never find a better factory restaurant in England. I couldn't believe how many vegetables were hidden under the seats.

I was really disappointed; I had worked against the odds without enough men to deliver the contract on time. Working long hours with a long drive there and back each day. My bosses had let me down by not providing support, and now the men were so pissed off that they were stealing vegetables from the client.

Being a proud man, I was determined to finish what I had started, and do a good job. I had contributed my skills and energy, and again failed to be recognised. This was not the way to treat me. So I had to make a decision: break out or break down. From that day I was never employed by anyone again.

From Navvy to Businessman

Working for others had made me feel trapped. Gone was the freedom of getting up and running across the fields back home in Ireland, making a living as and when I could. The daily grind of shifts and time clocks didn't appeal at all. I didn't mind hard work, but I wanted to do it on my own terms.

I now had a marketable skill – I decided to form a company and work for myself, offering plumbing and heating services. It was the sixties – thousands of houses still had outside toilets, few had bathrooms, and central heating was becoming the rage.

I set up Coventry Heating Engineers, running the business from the front room at home where a smart, second-hand polished oak desk and a new Remington typewriter took pride of place. Joan typed quotations and invoices between bringing up the boys.

Without blowing my own trumpet, I think I can say I had a good reputation as a hard worker who was fair and honest, and this created strong relationships with my clients. I treated people how I wanted to be treated myself, a valuable lesson learned from the Christian Brothers.

My brother Vincie was with me from the start, and then Doney recommended I take on a plumber named Andy Horton, who he had met on another job. Andy was a fantastic worker and an exceptional bloke. Small, wiry and as strong as an ox, you could give Andy any job and he would stick to it no matter how long it took. He'd come round to our house for a cup of tea and we'd travel to jobs together. For the next thirty years Andy was always there, always covered in grime, always with a fag in his mouth.

LITTLE FECKER!

I picked up small scale work, domestic plumbing and heating, quite easily, but I set myself the challenge of winning bigger contracts. An early attempt to get work at Alfred Herbert's failed, and the experience haunted me for a particular reason. I simply found it so hard to do more than one job in any one day.

On the day in question, I had an appointment with the chief engineer in Herbert's at 1.30pm. We had started a domestic central heating job in Bulkington in the morning. Vincie, Andy and I got stuck in and after four hours I asked the lady of the house if I could use her bathroom to get changed - I had a suit, shirt and tie in the van.

I waited in the massive reception at Herbert's like a lad waiting to have a dozen teeth out. In the middle of the room was a bronze bust of Alfred Herbert, one of the most famous engineers in the world. I didn't have a briefcase, just a pad and pen.

The works engineer collected me and before long my confidence was dented as he recognised me from having worked on site with another contractor. This was going to be tough.

We sat down. The engineer took a large book from the shelf and told me a certain employee had died. "I'm sorry to hear that," I said. He showed me where the man's name was entered in the book, and put a red line through it. "Oh yes", he explained, "we put a red line through all the employees when they pass away." I noticed a lot of red lines.

He closed the book, clearly not interested in discussing any opportunity for work. I had failed - I went back to the lady's bathroom to get changed for work. But being treated like that wasn't an experience I was prepared to repeat. I told myself, "never again!".

I had supplied skilled labour to Brightsides Ltd, so I had a little black book with a fair number of very good tradesmen. I set to work, and soon I had men working in Corby Steelworks, Hams Hall Power Station, a major food supply centre in Daventry, and various Birmingham car factories.

With the hours limited on some sites, I had to sniff around. I came across a company called Atlas, that specialised in sprinkler installation and big pipework. I approached a big Scotsman who had a caravan as his office, and introduced myself as Coventry Heating Engineers. He told me he was short of good welders. We talked rates, and the four lads I already had on site were over the moon to get overtime and weekend work at double pay.

Gaining confidence and courage to go into business can be a very long apprenticeship. The types of contract, systems and installations varied so much, and was of course very interesting; you did not have time to get bored. I loved the pipefitting, fabrication, welding and design elements of the work.

I think the costing was the reason I had not started up on my own sooner. In getting a contract, no matter how small, costing your materials is very important.

LITTLE FECKER!

To find work I advertised in the local press to quote for domestic central heating installations. I knew a fair bit about general plumbing, but I had never done a heating installation and had no idea about pricing one. I started to pick up as many tips as possible, phoning around heating suppliers and contractors I knew. This was where I got my first break.

I won two contracts within three weeks. I went to the council and enquired about bathroom conversions, heating and underground drainage. After doing two houses in Gadsby Street the council offered me as many houses as I could handle.

There was no turning back, I had to succeed. Determination creates luck, you can't sit around waiting for it to drop in your lap.

I phoned various heating companies and asked them how much it would cost to heat a two, three or four bedroomed house. Quite a few of them put the phone down, but I did manage to get some information and my next move was to visit plumbing and heating suppliers. This was to prove invaluable.

I called into a Coventry company called Ruymps. The manager, a Dublin man, said he would give me as much help as he could, if I opened an account and promised to buy the materials for at least my first heating contract from him. He promised me proper discounts and gave me the details of a retired heating contractor who would help me to quote for work. He recommended a good fitter, and I found a very good electrician called Keith Shilton.

The next important hurdle was the bank. If you are getting a month's credit for supply of materials then you must have money to pay on time, especially when you first start in business.

I sat down with Mr Stan Caldwell, the same Midland bank manager who gave me the £200 loan I needed for a deposit on my house in Nuneaton Road in 1960. Those were the days when bank managers were allowed to manage. I needed at least a £200 advance, I showed him four addresses of possible heating installations. There was no guarantee of work at any of them, but I had to show him something.

I was surprised and delighted when he said, "£200 isn't going to go very far." He gave me £400. He didn't even make reference to the fact that I was £112 in the red. (In those days, overdrawn accounts were written or typed in red ink on your statements.)

I walked on air to my old Bedford van in the car park – thank you again Mr Caldwell. When the right kind of people back you at the right time, you can fly!

Settling Down

Joan and I married in September 1959. The wedding was huge – two big families and lots of friends. We had our first son Sean in 1962. By the time Jimmy came along in 1965, I had started to feel that I needed roots, a solid base.

Travelling as a contractor is a different world to the ordinary man who works in a factory down the road

LITTLE FECKER!

every day. It gets into your blood - you become a mercenary. In the week you are the breadwinner, and you earn a good blowout at the weekends.

The problem in the game if you have a wife and family, is that you are forced to neglect them to make a living. You miss the importance of your children growing up, your wife becomes a work horse with no real support, while you are away, living a life of work, drink, work, drink.

September 1959 – with my lovely Joan

This is the type of life I lived, but was brave enough to get out. Do or die, we had to try. I have criticised myself for not being as good a father as I would like to have been. You see I did not have a father to teach me how to be a father. It's not an excuse but it makes me wonder.

CHE did well, but it was feast and famine – there were long periods when I didn't get a single day's plumbing work. But we had a lucky break one day when having a pint in my local, the Corner House in Bulkington with my brother-in-law, Desi Reilly. He pointed to a well-dressed couple across the room and said, "that's the bloke you should get to know, Noel." The man was Keith Thompson, and he was Chief Engineer at De Mulder & Sons, an animal products company on the outskirts of Nuneaton.

We won a contract at De Mulder's, and went from struggling to having twelve men working day and night. Nick de Mulder was a real gent, and he and wife Christine became great friends.

Years later, they gave my son Jimmy some work in the office, and when Nick noticed Jimmy had a cast in his eye he sent him straight to a specialist for an operation. Jimmy's eye has been perfect ever since, and we are all very grateful.

I managed to get a nice project, renovating and decorating a Chinese restaurant in Hinckley. It was quite a big job and by the time I was finished I was owed quite a lot of money. I was desperately short of cash at the time so one lunchtime, as I was driving

LITTLE FECKER!

past the restaurant with Joan, Sean and Jimmy in the car, I decided to call in and see the owner. A waiter told me the boss was out but would return later.

I had decided I wouldn't leave without my money, so I waited for him. After a while I decided that it didn't look good to be just sitting there without buying anything, so although I only had a couple of pounds I fetched Joan and the boys in from the car and we shared three portions of chips, which was all I could afford.

We finished the chips and there was no sign of the boss, so I paid the small bill and tried to accept the fact I wasn't getting any money that day. As we all rose to leave the table, the owner returned and, seeing me, he rushed over, shook my hand and called to the waiter, 'No charge for this man, everything he had is on the house'. Fortunately I saw the funny side of missing out on a slap-up lunch, and I was paid for the work shortly afterwards.

Doney tipped me off that British Rail were looking for someone to fulfil a parcel delivery contract, so I decided to branch out. British Rail had many more deliveries than drivers, so I borrowed a few quid and bought four second hand vans. I took on a couple of friends, and soon had a fast and anonymous parcel delivery business. I had to keep it low key; it wouldn't help prospects if CHE's clients were to discover I was moonlighting!

Goodbye Daddy

In 1966 I hired a minibus and on the day England won the World Cup I took some of the family – Joan, Sean and Jimmy, Daddy and Joan, Doney, his wife Norma and children Danny and Donna, and Vincie over to Dublin. We listened to the radio commentary as we drove up the A5 to Holyhead in blistering sunshine.

We rented a nice big house in Ballymun, Dublin, then went on to stay in a lighthouse at Malahide. For me, it was a special treat both to take my wife and sons to Ireland for the first time, and to be back in the "old country" with Daddy.

We visited all the old haunts, including a Dolly Heffernan's, a pub near the quarry where Tom Traynor had saved my life when I nearly drowned as a boy. Imagine my surprise when in the pub, playing music, was Tom's son, my old friend Davie Traynor!

Davie had a rare talent for the music – he could play any instrument. The gathered crowd, crammed into the small bar, begged Davie to play "the Marching Band". Davie stood with his back to the wooden counter and started to drum on it with his hands, quietly at first then progressively louder. It sounded exactly as if fifty marching drummers were coming down the road! Then with just his lips he added the sound of bugles and trumpets. The sound grew really loud then faded away as if the band had marched past the pub and away down the road. Everyone roared – a fantastic skill and a treasured memory.

LITTLE FECKER!

I was in my element, and having a super holiday. Daddy had been really keen to make the trip and was having a fantastic time. But unfortunately, and unknown to me, Daddy was seriously ill.

And for over a year after our wonderful holiday, Daddy grew steadily worse. As it turned out, stepmother Joan and my sisters knew how ill Daddy was, and had known even while we were in Dublin. They knew it would hit me hard, so they said nothing. And me being the supreme optimist, I didn't see what was coming.

But I was suddenly thrown into the role of "head of the family". This role would normally fall to the eldest child. Back in Ireland, with Daddy away and Mammy ill, Maureen, the eldest, would be in charge. But when Maureen moved to England, and with Benny and Vincie at work, Rita became the head of the family.

Now, suddenly, Daddy became very ill and was rushed into hospital in Birmingham. I had just started my own business, and this gave me the flexibility to take time away from work and drive back and forward, to get updates on how Daddy was.

Only weeks earlier, I had taken Daddy to look at a small factory near where we lived. The owners were winding up their hosiery business, and I was very excited – even though I had no capital, I had a plan in my head. The plan was to get Daddy away from the Sterling Metals and the smog and grime that was coating his lungs and chest and killing him.

When we first came to England, Daddy had told me that a close friend, a fellow Irishman, had begged him to go and work in Forestry in Canada. Daddy didn't go but the friend did, and he became a millionaire. I often recalled the conversation, and couldn't help but think of the wide-open spaces, and the clean fresh air that Daddy might have been breathing all these years.

What I had in mind was a home improvement, bathroom, plumbing and DIY parts business. I showed Daddy the long yard at the rear of the factory and told him how I could imagine him in charge of six big bricked bays, full of sand, gravel and cement. He would be mixing with the customers and out in the fresh air.

Then, just a few weeks later, on a Thursday morning, I got a message, asking for a senior member of the family to call in and see the consultant before visiting Daddy. I did this without feeling unduly concerned. But the surgeon sat me down and showed me a piece of paper with a drawing of a pair of lungs. He said, "we have operated on your Dad's right lung, and I am sorry to say we can't save him." He took a pen and drew a large black dot on the lung, and said "that's where the problem is."

I'll never know how I got to the ward without falling over. My insides were upside down, my legs were like jelly. Daddy's bed had been moved to the near end of the ward by the big clock. For the first time ever I put my arm around his shoulder and caressed his face, I can remember saying, "God bless you Daddy, you'll be all right".

LITTLE FECKER!

On the journey back to Nuneaton, I kept thinking "we're losing the head of the family". I really didn't want to live without Daddy, it hurt me so hard not having him at home for ten years from age four to fourteen. And now we were losing him forever.

I looked at several of the big trees on the lanes on the way home, and several times I seriously considered driving my car into one of them. Thank God I didn't; I would have been a selfish coward and brought nothing but further grief on my family.

Daddy was to pass away peacefully a few days later, with all the family around him. But that wasn't the end of the tragedy.

I drove home from the hospital after saying goodbye to Daddy, dropping my dear sister Rose at her home in Tamworth, then taking brother Pat to Coventry. When I got home to Joan, Rose had phoned. While she had been with us at the hospital, Rose's husband Derek had taken their two boys John, 6, and Michael, aged 2, to the barber for a haircut. They had come out of the barber's at 1:30pm – the time of Daddy's death - and little Michael had dashed out between two parked cars and was hit a glancing blow by the mirror of a passing car. He was taken to the Good Hope Hospital in Sutton Coldfield and passed away peacefully next day.

We had no choice other than to comfort ourselves in the certainty that Daddy and Michael were meant to accompany one anther on the journey to heaven.

Daddy had passed away on 21st December 1967, little Michael the next day. After Christmas, we had Daddy's funeral in the morning and Michael's in the afternoon. My heart went out to Rose and Derek; what an awful double tragedy and terrible loss.

Danny Kelly. A great man, sadly missed.

Stepping Up

Coventry Industrial Pipework

Daddy's death hit me very hard. But I had to get back to work, and feed my growing family. The domestic heating business was good, but the idea of providing pipework services in Coventry's petrochemical companies and car factories was tugging at me.

At the end of 1973, Fate stepped in. Driving home in pouring rain, I saw a man at a bus stop getting drenched to the skin. I stopped - in those days such acts of kindness were allowed - the man turned out to be Ron Fenton, a neighbour who was Facilities Engineer at Alfred Herbert's. He was grateful for the lift, and asked how business was going.

Ron suggested that with my skill and experience I should be taking on high budget commercial work, not busting a gut on small domestic jobs. He offered to introduce me to the decision makers at Herbert's. It was a life-changing meeting in the rain, thanks Ron!

As a result, in 1974 I started a new company, Coventry Industrial Pipework (CIP). The breakthrough into the industrial side came when Ron invited me to quote for work on a high pressure heating system at Herbert's Red Lane Works. We won this contract and additional work of around £15,000 – big money in those days.

I'd had no formal business training, but I suppose my business apprenticeship goes back a long way. I had no direction, no education, no role models and no guidance. I had to rely on the experience I'd gained up to that point from all the jobs I'd had growing up.

Though I've always had the Irish gift of the gab - Joan used to call me "Rattle-pants." I like to think of myself as a good listener. I had met a lot of people and learned from all of them. After all my experience, I suddenly found myself in charge, the business equivalent of "famous". I was *somebody*.

I felt completely out of my depth talking to educated engineers about pipework systems that ran the length and breadth of huge industrial plants, but I got on well and they seemed interested in what I had to offer, which was first and foremost a commitment to deliver on my promises.

Key to success in the short and long term was that I quickly built an incredible team of lads. Not only was each hardworking and very talented technically, but they were all great characters. There was a fantastic atmosphere in the CIP workshop and on any site when the team was together.

Andy Horton was still with me, of course. Freddie Hinch, a Dublin lad, worked for one of my competitors for some time. I advertised for skilled men and was delighted when Freddie knocked on my door - he was a top quality tradesman. His brothers Liam and Richard, and his son Eddie also worked for us. These were joined by Tony Stringer, Terry Fox, Gary Manning, Brian Burn and Jimmy Caffrey.

LITTLE FECKER!

Fred spent 22 years with CIP, running the works and handling specialised jobs like inductors for Morris Engines, test beds and pipework for Rolls Royce. He was an excellent fitter welder, and also a very artistic designer. Once, in a quiet spell, I gave him a big pile of scrap metal, and he designed and built a unique stainless steel knight, which stood almost 3 metres tall. We called it "Mr CIP"; Rolls Royce borrowed him for open days, and he appeared in the Courtaulds National magazine, which went all round the world in the industry. I believe, and hope, that "Mr CIP" still stands proudly in Fred's daughter's garden.

The Kelly brothers worked at CIP. Benny, Vincie, Doney, Pat and Paul, and Doney's son Danny, a smashing lad who died at just 40, a tragic loss. I didn't treat my family any differently to the other lads; I didn't need to – they just got on with the work and the craic.

Benny had an excellent engineering brain. He worked at Carrier's for years, but joined me as soon as I set up CIP and was in charge of our first major contract. At one point he left, to take a job with Chrysler after they took over the Humber factory; Chrysler set up an internal maintenance department - offering 25% higher pay than contractors could afford - and creamed off a lot of the top tradesmen. I lost Benny, but he was bored without the variety and the lads, so he came back!

He was five feet ten tall and very broad and solid. People in the town used to call him Rocky Marciano, my son Sean called him Desperate Dan. He was a heavy drinker but never fell over, and if he hit someone he only needed to hit them once. He never started a fight in his life but they used to come looking for him, especially little guys full of drink.

Benny was the main instigator of all the Kellys getting into the pipework business. After his engineering brain and ability got him a good job with Carriers, Benny began to draw us in, away from trench digging. He got Doney in first, then me, then Vincie who had carried on travelling for some time on his own. So we have a lot to thank Benny for. He never went to college – he could just look at the drawings and tell the engineers what was wrong with them. Benny designed special hangers for hot pipes to be suspended in the air and improved their flexibility for expansion. We all had it a bit – once we saw someone do something once we could do it ourselves.

Benny was forced to retire after a stroke and came to live with us for a year during his recovery. The family took it in turns to look after him - his marriage had split up; and we didn't want him put in a home. He died three years after his stroke; he was only 56. When I took Benny to a specialist he said we'd left it too late - his blood pressure was sky high. The GP admitted he hadn't checked Benny's blood pressure for two years, even though he'd been going in with headaches. It turned out he'd already had several little strokes.

It was a shock to lose Benny so young, but he was a great man who'd enjoyed life to the full.

LITTLE FECKER!

Pat, Doney and I all liked to dabble in the horses, but Vincie was in another class. He used to do a daily betting shop run for all the lads. If he went missing we knew where he was. Vincie worked with CIP for the rest of his life, even after a double heart bypass.

We took a grand young Irish lad, Mick Brennan, on an apprenticeship. Mick was blind in one eye but was game for anything – he was desperate to qualify as a welder. Then a doctor told him the sight in his good eye was failing. I had to look after his sight, so I took him away from welding and moved him into pipe-fitting. He'd get fed up and disappear for weeks at a time, then I'd arrive on site and there would be Mick, welding! He'd turn up out of the blue and tell the lads "Noel says I can weld". He was such a canny lad, it was hard to say no to him, but I had to.

As much as he loved welding, Mick loved the gang. His brother had been killed crossing the road, and Vincie was like a big brother to Mick; they were inseparable.

So Mick was a great lad, but his good eye was getting worse, and I could tell that this was worrying him. Then one summer's day he was a passenger in a car, and had his arm hanging out the window. Another car came alongside and smashed into Mick, wrecking his arm. Some of the lads thought it had been deliberate, but Mick assured me it was an accident, though the other car had driven off.

Mick was told he would struggle with manual work, and would also have to give up his beloved karate. I met him for a drink – he was worried he was losing his sight, and was quite depressed. But I kept finding jobs for him – he came into the yard most days, and the last time I saw him he was doing some painting and having a real laugh with a couple of the lads.

Mick's best mate and another close friend had both committed suicide using a dressing gown belt over the bathroom door. Mick chose that same route out. It was so very sad.

His wake was a real Irish affair - massive. Mick had so many close friends – the CIP team and the Kellys saw him as a brother, and we sent him off in the style he deserved.

* * *

As the business expanded, we were approached to look at some very high tech work in the petrochemical industry. I decided it was time to recruit a top quality engineer, and found the perfect man - Bernard Brookes.

Bernard had a fantastic engineering brain – it was clear at the interview and he showed it many many times over his years with the company, both to me and to senior engineers at our clients. Not only was he a brilliant technician, but he was honest, hardworking. There's no question that without him CIP would not have been the great success it became.

Bernard was very fit, and swam a couple of miles every morning before work. He was such a good swimmer that England contenders who used

LITTLE FECKER!

Coventry's Olympic-length pool would quiz him on his approach and technique.

One year Bernard went to the Dominican Republic on holiday, and my son Sean was in the same hotel the following year. When he was warned not to swim out over the reef because there were jellyfish, Sean mentioned that he knew a keen swimmer who had been there the previous year. "Oh, that must have been Mr Brookes! Yes, he nearly died!"

Sean was flabbergasted – Bernard had said nothing. But the story went like this: Bernard swam beyond the reef, and was hit in the chest by a Portuguese Man of War. Somehow, he managed to get back over the reef, swim 100 metres to shore, and crawl onto the beach with the jellyfish still wrapped round him. A big guy picked Bernard up, threw him over his shoulder and ran 200 metres up the beach, through the hotel and out into the street, where a taxi driver took them to the hospital and saved Bernard's life.

When I told Bernard what Sean had told me, he just laughed. "Oh, yes. It wasn't that bad, really." Bernard was a modest, unassuming and talented man, with a dry sense of humour and a sharp, analytical brain.

Much of my early success – and survival – at CIP came as a result of solid friendships I had made in previous jobs. I have to be grateful

I had worked with a super Yorkshire man named Bert Timmins at Sulzer Bros, and Bert had given me some small bits of work when I started CHE. He was now established at Courtaulds Little Heath Works in Coventry, and his contractors had more work than they could handle in run up to Christmas. Bert remarked to Arthur Wincott, the maintenance manager, "I can't cover all the small jobs. Why not get Kelly in to quote for them? He used to work for us and he's great".

I was very short of work, and it's incredible how you can be lucky or unlucky; Arthur called me just as I was going out, I might have missed the opportunity of a lifetime if I'd missed that call. Arthur asked how I was doing for work and I said I was just managing to keep my chin above the water. He invited me over, and introduced me to maintenance foreman Brian Bennett and his colleague Sammy Lynch, a little Dublin man.

They took me on a tour around several chemical plants and asked me to quote for 20 different jobs. I had my notebook, and was having to write down and spell chemical words I'd never heard before. This was when I first faced my lack of education. It was so nearly very embarrassing, but I managed to get round it by *pretending* to write.

Brian and Sammy both knew the plant inside out and knew all the names – it was a nightmare. At one point Brian looked over my shoulder to check I was getting it down properly, and the page – the first in an empty book - was blank apart from a rough sketch of the pipework I had drawn. I just tapped my head, winked and nodded –Brian seemed happy enough.

Apart from calling Brian a couple of times to check spellings, I did the twenty quotes from memory, and I won all the jobs. It wasn't our first industrial contract, but it was to kick-start CIP – we worked in Courtaulds for over 20 years.

In the early days we didn't make a lot of money, as I didn't really know how to quote properly, but being on site gives you opportunities to pick up work. One day I was walking by the canal with Sammy Lynch, and he said "Noel, you see that fella over there? If you want to get work on this site, that's the man you need to get acquainted with."

The man was Gerald Shiers. Gerald was a very laid back Coventry guy – he didn't stand any messing about. He was kind and easy to work with because he knew the game and knew contractors – duff contractors didn't last on chemical plants, especially not with Gerald around. We had mutual professional respect. If things didn't go right he soon had me on the mat, he was a good man and his company came first.

Gerald and I had a mutual love of Coventry City Football Club, and Bernard got on with Gerald like a house on fire; he appreciated a fully qualified Mech.E who spoke his language.

All the Courtaulds engineers recognised and appreciated Bernard's skill and qualifications, and CIP took off then in a big way. Thanks to Bernard, top end specialised work was to be our future.

I should give myself a bit of credit for hiring the right men. Bernard, as technical design engineer, quoted the major projects. Once they were won and came into the workshop, it was my job to ensure they were fulfilled and shipped to the site, then to be on site until everything was installed.

As CIP moved into petrochemical work, Bernard pushed me to invest in the lads to upgrade their skills. I spent thousands of pounds on their training – a great investment. I had pulled together and now managed a team of highly professional craftsmen. And, also important, all the men were fully qualified in Health and Safety practice... In theory, at least.

Health and Safety? Our Speciality!

Brian Jack was a contracts engineer in Courtaulds who was well known for being very strict on health and safety. A big job was coming up and we were favourites to get it, but another company on the Courtaulds site in Derby played clever: they stuck a load of health and safety posters all over the walls inside their works hut, including the inside of the door, then pushed the door open when they saw Brian walking past. Drawn by their attention to health and safety, Brian went in to say hello, and ended up inviting them to quote for the big job.

I knew CIP would be the best team for the job. I also knew we would be in trouble if we didn't get it. I called Alan Potts, a Courtaulds design draughtsman I had known for some years, now working at Spondon. I asked Alan his opinion of our competitor for the

LITTLE FECKER!

£650,000 contract. He told me they had given Brian a sob story, saying they had no work, and had men with families and kids to feed. Alan thought Brian might be swayed by this, and suggested I tell Brian a similar story. But it wasn't a story – it was true!

Brian said he'd call by our office after 6pm, but warned me that there was a £45,000 difference between our quote and our competitor's. Bernard didn't want to stay late to talk to Brian – it was Tuesday. But I knew Bernard's presence was key - he might be able to convince Brian, so I persuaded him to stay. I didn't think to ask why Tuesday was important.

The meeting was going well; I described to Brian the services we had supplied over 20 years. We knew the plant inside out, we were on the doorstep, and we had turned out on many occasions in the middle of the night to keep the plant running. I also followed Alan's important advice, and told Brian my men had wives, kids and mortgages.

We reached a crucial negotiation point - the price. I was just about to reduce our quote, when there was a weird scratching sound in the office, that got louder and louder. Bernard knew exactly what it was, but never blinked. Brian and I were really confused. Then a huge lobster crawled out from under Bernard's desk and across the floor, dragging a brown paper bag behind it.

Ah yes. Tuesday. I had forgotten. Forgotten that Bernard, a creature of habit, would buy a live lobster from Coventry's fish market every Tuesday morning, for his tea that night. So here we were, in the final stages of discussing the biggest contract we'd ever quoted for, and a lobster was chasing our client around the office!

Suddenly, Brian really had to go – he got up and thanked us for our time. I tried to break the tension with a joke - Brian didn't laugh. Fortunately though, he did give us the job. A milestone in the company's history, nearly wrecked by a lobster!

On one job in the early days, we had lowered Andy Horton into a big hole to weld a pipe fifteen feet below ground. I'll never forget Andy, holding all his welding gear, hanging upside down by chains round his ankles. Totally fearless, totally mad. twenty years later at Courtaulds, such a *creative* approach to getting the job done was simply not allowed.

One of our men, Terry Fox, was an excellent tradesman, fit, strong and a terrific worker. But Terry was also a sun worshipper - difficult in a chemical plant, where you are required to wear overalls. As soon as the sun came out, off came Terry's overall, shirt and trousers – he'd be wearing shorts underneath. The Courtaulds engineers loved Terry, but health and safety was paramount, and on many occasions Terry nearly got us chucked off the site.

One day an engineer, Dave Lumley, was touring the site with a Health and Safety inspector. They came round the corner to find Terry forty feet up in the air with one foot on the highest part of the scaffolding –

not even on the platform - leaning across pipes with two spanners trying to stop a leak. Dave, horrified, tapped the bottom of the scaffold to attract Terry's attention. That didn't work so Dave picked up a stone and banged the scaffold, then shouted "Terry, stop!"

Terry's reply was to the point: "You can fuck off – I'm going to stop this leak before I go anywhere!" To make things worse, Terry was wearing shorts, a straw hat, and no shirt. I was up in front of the hierarchy and got a right telling off! But Terry was a brilliant bloke to have working for you. He was like a weightlifter, and you couldn't find a harder worker.

One afternoon our lads were out of harm's way, on a break in our tea hut. Tony Stringer, a top fitter-welder, was leaning out of the window looking at the canal, and our driver Charlie Lynch was stirring tea. For a bit of fun, Charlie took the spoon out of the red-hot tea and pressed it into Tony's exposed kidneys. Tony screamed and bashed his head on the wooden window frame, turned round and hit Charlie. Liam Hinch jumped in to stop Tony from hitting him again.

Gerald Shiers was passing and heard the kerfuffle. As he opened the door the fight spilled out of the hut into the workshop, almost knocking Gerald flying. What followed was like a scene from a western – seven lads battering hell out of each other.

Two miles down the road at CIP, I was in my office. My secretary Val came in, "Liam Hinch is in reception." The look on her face told me something was wrong. Liam had four cuts on his face and a big black eye. "It wasn't my fault, it was Charlie Lynch!" he babbled.

I calmed Liam down and went to pour him a coffee, but before I could get back to him and get the facts, the phone rang. It was Gerald Shiers.

Fortunately, Gerald took the view that as the fight was in my workshop, not his, there was no need to take it any higher.

For all the fun and games, CIP had a fantastic safety record - sixteen years without a single claim.

Ned the Entertainer

With CIP doing well, I was able to entertain loyal clients. Each year I would arrange a company dinner dance, where it was my pleasure to host an evening of excellent food and entertainment at one of Coventry's top hotels. One year had gone particularly well and I decided to invite my family to celebrate with us at the dinner dance. It was a very proud moment.

I also enjoyed a good relationship with my close neighbours at Coventry City, where I became a Vice President and attended home matches and monthly sportsman's evenings, with after dinner speakers including boxing commentator Reg Gutteridge, Danny Blanchflower, and Derek Dougan, a real character who became a good friend.

With CIP doing well, I treated myself to a personalised registration number for my car. As I was Managing Director of Coventry Industrial Pipework, I

LITTLE FECKER!

thought the title 'Mr CIP' would be appropriate, and be an opportunity to get free PR for the business.

I bought 'MRC 1P' and re-spaced the letters to represent who I was. The local car dealer arranged press coverage when I picked up my new car, but a keen young bobby caught up with me very soon afterwards, and charged me with displaying an *illegible* number plate. I was aware that moving the letter 'C' a quarter-inch to the right was, strictly speaking, against the rules, but it was clear what the plate said, and my transgression was nothing compared to some of the examples I see today.

The judge threw the case out of court, saying, "The registration is not *illegible*; it is quite clearly MRC 1P. It is simply incorrectly spaced."

This embarrassed the police and I guess they decided to embarrass me in return; a police car followed me onto client premises just two days after the court case, lights flashing and sirens blaring. The same police officer got out, a huge grin on his face as he charged me with displaying an *incorrectly spaced* number plate.

I was fined £25 and ordered to display my plate correctly, which cost me another £10. The pettiness of the police appealed to the national press, as the story appeared on page 3 of the Sun newspaper under the headline "Naughty Noel's Number's Up". Some people have called me Naughty Noel ever since.

Infatuation: Nuneaton Borough Football Club

From spectator to director - joining the Board

In the 1960's and early 70's I had laid the foundations of a business and a family. Sean and Jimmy were growing up, and daughters Nicky and Trish were born in 1969 and 1975.

Joan, like me, was from a big family. Her sisters Nancy, Betty, Alice and Janet all loved to laugh like Joan did, and I got on very well with my brothers in law over many years, drinking regularly with Betty, Alice and Janet's husbands Ken, John and Ken.

We would play cards in the Pheasant pub in Camp Hill on a Saturday night and have a real laugh. We would buy a huge pile of fish and chips on the way back to Betty's, where the wives and kids, eventually Betty's seven, our four, Alice's two and Janet's four, would wait for us to come in and dive on the food.

Always one for a laugh, a couple of times I appeared at Betty's door in a mask –a gorilla, which got me into big trouble as one of the sisters was pregnant and got quite a scare, and another time a Larry Grayson mask I bought in Skegness, that was supposed to make people laugh, but was somehow even creepier.

My business grew and I was financially stable. We moved from the semi-detached house I had bought when we got married into a lovely detached bungalow. For the first time I was able to buy a new car, and not just any car but a shiny Jaguar in the most gorgeous shade of blue.

We took a family holiday at a British seaside resort every summer, but a nice little pools win, about £3,500, meant that Joan and I were able to spend an amazing fortnight in the Seychelle Islands. I continued to enjoy socialising with my clients, many of whom shared my love of football.

But I continued to work very hard. And my twice-daily drive past Coventry City's Highfield Road stadium – just two hundred yards from CIP's offices - had whetted my appetite for football. On the odd Saturday afternoons when I wasn't working, I would go to watch a game at Highfield Road. Jimmy Hill had arrived in Coventry like a breath of fresh air, and everyone was infected with Sky Blue fever. So I joined the Vice President's Club at Coventry City and entertained there, at monthly evening events as well as watching as many games as I could.

They were good times, but my growing infatuation with football was to lead to an obsession that would turn my life in a whole new direction.

The club that was to receive the benefit of my interest, energy and passion, directly for ten years and indirectly for the rest of my life, was not in Coventry but much closer to home. At a ground called Manor Park, Nuneaton had its own proud and moderately successful semi-professional football club. Where top-flight-professional City seemed inaccessible, hidden from the public behind locked gates, Nuneaton

Borough Football Club - *'The Boro'* – was friendly, open, much more suited to a curious young Irishman.

I had made my home in Nuneaton and visited Manor Park a few times - you could say I was bribed to watch my first-ever Boro match, in December 1953. The FA Cup replay against Queen's Park Rangers was one of the biggest games in the club's history. We were building houses at Camp Hill when Fred Pallet came round and told the whole gang we could go and give the Boro our support. He said he would check we were there, and if we stayed for the whole game he would pay us for the afternoon as if we'd worked. It was a no-brainer!

We stood on the Beaumont Road grass bank; the ground was packed, the atmosphere superb. Boro lost 2-1, but I vividly remember my enjoyment, a feeling I was to repeat many years later. My obsession truly started that day.

Twelve years later, I was among 22,000 jammed into the ground for the FA Cup visit of Rotherham. I was on good form - I had won £400 on the horses on my way to the match, a nice sum in 1966.

It was a wet, mucky day but the Boro turned in a great performance to earn a replay. I joined my mates for a celebration in the social club. There we were, a happy group sitting on some old wooden barrels they used to have for seats, having a good old time on my winnings. That memory often flashed through my mind years later, when I would spend endless hours among friends and fans at the social club bar.

LITTLE FECKER!

In 1975, I started going regularly to the Boro, to have a drink with Doney in the social club. I began to get to know a few of the blokes in there. It was quite a friendly place and, more and more, I would call in on match nights for a pint.

That was how I was first approached about getting involved. The steward, Frank Parker, collared me and told me that the club was looking for businessmen to join the board. "They're desperate for help," he said.

It didn't hit me that he was suggesting I get involved myself - I had never imagined that someone like me could actually help to run a football club. I didn't know what sort of person did such things; I just assumed they weren't like me.

Doney said, "You've worked seven days a week all your life, why don't you take a break, give it a try? Something different - you might enjoy it." It's ironic that this "break" was to take up as much of my time as work ever did!

I didn't say yes, but I didn't say no. Frank took my silence as a yes, and had a word in the right ear. Before long, a formal approach came from director Ken Peal and chairman David Tinney. I met them and got a bit interested. Things were going well at CIP, so I mulled the idea over. Before long, I was sitting in the directors' box. My life was about to move in a new direction - and would never be the same again.

I was officially co-opted on to the Boro board in October 1976. For a while I took very much a back seat. I just enjoyed being part and parcel of the football club. It gave me a new interest and the more I got involved, the more enjoyable it became.

Just a couple of months after joining the board, I celebrated my 40th birthday with a trip to Lincoln to see them play Nuneaton in the second round of the FA Cup. Lincoln were in the Football League and managed by future England manager Graham Taylor, so this was my first real taste of a giant-killing opportunity – it took me back to the games against QPR and Rotherham, the crowds' passion of 1953 and 1966 was still in my heart. And at a deeper, more personal level, I went back to my days in Ireland – the poor young boy up against the mean farmer, the Christian Brothers, and the Garda.

It was a bitter December day, and the Sincil Bank pitch was covered in snow – even though these were the days before underground heating and crowd safety issues, we were amazed that the referee gave the go-ahead for the game to be played.

The Nuneaton team slipped and slid ridiculously for ninety minutes, and trudged off the pitch as 6-0 losers, in what is still Nuneaton's heaviest ever cup defeat. After the game the manager told the press he'd chosen the wrong length stud for the conditions. I felt he was being harsh on himself!

Unfortunately, while the directors were being entertained in the Lincoln boardroom, a small minority of Nuneaton "fans" were venting their frustration on the streets of Lincoln – I was to hear

LITTLE FECKER!

from reporters that a crowd chanting "you won't forget Nuneaton" had attacked cars, shops and people in the town.

The club had chartered a train to take fans to the game. Lincoln has a train track running literally through the city centre streets. As the Boro train set off, a crowd of Lincoln fans – armed with bricks and bottles - exacted their revenge: the Boro fans travelled home that night in windy freezing conditions in carriages with hardly a window intact.

News of these events spoiled my birthday far more than the result, but fortunately such incidents were very rare in the years ahead. On the whole, the Boro fans were a happy, well-behaved bunch, and for the next ten years, working with the club was a very pleasant experience.

Becoming Chairman

For a good while, about a year, I was blissfully unaware that behind the happy façade, there were massive problems lurking in the shadows.

The first warning sign came when the VAT man served a writ on the club, for about £3,000. Sitting at my desk at CIP, I got a frantic call from the club's Office Manager Arthur Moss, saying, "They've come to close the club down." He said no-one could get hold of the chairman, Tinney, and the VAT man wasn't taking no for an answer. So I left work in Coventry and, after stopping off at the bank to pick up a bankers' draft for £3,000 from my own personal account, drove straight to Leicester to the VAT office. I paid the outstanding bill, and kept Boro in business – it seemed the obvious thing to do. I didn't realise at the time, but it was to be the first of many personal cheques I would issue to ensure the football club's survival.

Tinney didn't reappear, and at the next board meeting it was proposed that I become Chairman. It came as a complete surprise – no-one had suggested it to me in advance of the meeting. But I'd already felt the buzz of saving the club – I was hungry, I could see that I could make something great happen here – and I wanted more. I said yes without a second's hesitation and was elected by a unanimous vote.

Looking back, everything was going my way, I was on top of the world. I had come from nothing to be a big fish in Nuneaton, a much bigger pool than the old crossroads in Kilbride!

Running Nuneaton Borough Football Club was very quickly to take over my life, and events off the pitch eventually became more important than those on it. But before all that, we had some great football to watch, in an incredible, indelible decade when football was all that mattered...

I couldn't help but be inspired Jimmy Hill's achievements at Coventry City in the 1960's. With a range of innovations he made visiting Highfield Road a bigger experience than just a match, and set the club up for 34 years of uninterrupted top-flight football.

LITTLE FECKER!

I set myself a plan, to pursue and achieve:

> Team success in FA Cup and League competitions by choosing good players, paying decent salaries, and having a good manager.

> Increased club revenue, to be able to pay players and keep the ground in good condition, via sponsors, a lottery, club shop and astute transfers.

> Prestige for the club by treating visitors well, running charity events, Italian trips, bonfires and social events.

> Looking after the club's assets – its players and, though the club didn't own it yet, the ground.

My longer term aims were to take the club to an FA Trophy final at Wembley, to reach the 3rd Round of the FA Cup and play a top flight team, and to one day see Nuneaton Borough play in the Football League – a feat rarely achieved by non-league clubs in those days, before the introduction of the pyramid system, and long before automatic promotion.

Being a football fan is like riding a roller-coaster. Ups and downs, excitement, anticipation, hair-raising moments, times when your heart is in your mouth and your stomach is full of butterflies. Just when you think you have reached the highest high, soccer has that knack of hauling you down into the depths.

But that is what makes the game so fascinating. Being in charge of a football club magnifies all those feelings: when the team wins, you're right in the middle of the greatest buzz of celebration I've ever known. You suffer every defeat as hard as any fan on the terraces, then you have to watch the effect on your players, your colleagues and the club's bank balance!

I took over as Boro chairman in May 1977. When it came to soccer administration, I was very green, but I had been green about pipework and engineering, yet built a successful and well-respected business. I was prepared to give it a go.

After years of relative obscurity, I felt like I was suddenly catapulted into the limelight. Something that started as an opportunity to help a football club, to provide entertainment for a group of local people, took me by surprise.

The role of Chairman brought with it a certain status. All of a sudden the local newspapers – the Nuneaton Tribune and Coventry Telegraph – were interested in what I had to say. And I took advantage of that – I knew that getting stories about the football club on the back page of the local rags – and quite often on the front – would create profile for the club, and generate interest and, eventually, increase crowds at the matches.

That would not only increase revenue for a struggling outfit, but further improve the atmosphere in the ground, which was already pretty good. And this would raise the entertainment levels for the fans.

Personally, I was being recognised by strangers in the street, which appealed to my love of an audience. In social situations, friends who had never shown any appetite for football - lads I had drunk with for years who clearly preferred rugby and cricket - were suddenly taking an interest in what was going on, both on and off the pitch. I loved it – there were some great stories to tell, as I hope you're about to find out!

So, the beginning of a new role, a new career: football Chairman. It was the beginning of the summer break, but I got straight down to work. The Noel Kelly who had won awards for the state of his bed in the Army wasn't going to invite fans to stand on terraces with weeds on them!

I recruited a gang of hard-working volunteers, rolled up my sleeves, and together we made much-needed repairs to the pitch, stands and terraces. The Nuneaton Evening Tribune announced my arrival as Chairman by printing a photograph of me up a ladder, painting the goalposts. The picture looked completely posed, and mates in the pub pulled my leg about it, but the reporter had turned up to interview me, earlier than arranged, and his eagle-eyed photographer had spotted me and grabbed the opportunity.

It was a busy and successful summer. But the 1977-78 season had not even kicked off when I received a double blow; our player-manager Stan Bennett - a great midfielder who had played 428 games in 15 years with Walsall - suffered a badly broken leg in a pre-season friendly.

NOEL KELLY

Hands-on, working hard, the Kelly way!

Bennett was in leg irons for months. He had moulded a decent squad together, but it as clear he couldn't fulfil his role of managing the team while on crutches. It was a tough decision but we had to let him go – we had a long talk and he agreed it was for the best. His assistant Stan Marshall took the reins and was soon leading us to FA Cup victory over Hednesford. The First Round proper brought a home tie against League side Oxford United, the first of many "big days" for me as chairman.

7,759 fans, Boro's biggest attendance for 11 years, watched the game. Top-flight neighbours Leicester City didn't have a game that day, so our gate was swelled by a Leicester contingent, some, memorably, with hair dyed in blue and white quarters. our colours as well as Leicester's!

We were contacted by the Oxford United secretary, Jim Hunt, who told us that a contingent of Oxford fans would cause trouble if they were able to. Jim came to meet us at Manor Park, and we showed him our plans to erect fences to segregate the fans. Jim thought that would work, and he suggested kicking off at 2pm rather than 3pm, so the fans would leave after the game in daylight. When we announced the 2pm kick-off, many of our fans believed that Oxford had criticised our floodlights, but this wasn't the case.

So, ahead of the game I dipped my hand in my pocket for some wire fencing and had some CIP lads come over to erect sturdy segregation barriers – a new sight on football pitches back then.

The Oxford fans did plan to cause trouble that day. Somehow they had learned about our fences, and they turned up armed - with wire cutters! Fortunately our stalwart stewards, helped by the fences, managed to keep the handful of idiots at bay.

The day ended perfectly, as we emerged 2-0 winners. We even got an added benefit of kicking off at 2pm; for much of the afternoon our early victory over League opposition was the leading story on local and national media outlets

Here I was, Chairman for less than six months, and Boro were hailed as giant-killers with a place in the FA Cup Second Round.

We were drawn at home to Tilbury, a side from London's Docklands who were in a league below our level and should have provided a not-too-stiff task. But after our victory against Oxford, we should have known that football isn't like that!

My Irish luck deserted me, and a grass divot scored a goal. After just 10 minutes, the ball hit a clump of turf in the penalty area and deflected off goalkeeper Bob Knight's shoulder and into the back of our net. We equalised, but a blunder in the second-half handed Tilbury a 2-1 result. A golden chance of reaching the Third Round, and a tie against Stoke City, tossed away. Coming so close so soon just fuelled my desire and my belief that we could and would achieve my dream of playing one of the top teams one day.

To compensate, we had the honour of being invited to take part in the semi-professional Anglo-Italian Tournament. Then Stan Marshall announced he didn't want to continue as manager. We received 47 applications for the job and appointed Ian McKechnie, a former Arsenal and Hull goalkeeper who wanted to get into management.

Ian impressed us at his interview and began well - three wins and three draws. Then I received a phone call from his wife in Hull to say Ian was no longer our manager. He cited "private and personal reasons" in the press, but didn't speak to me. He had left his digs in Nuneaton in a hurry, caught a taxi all the way to Hull, and we never saw him again.

From my experience in business, I had very quickly learned the importance of getting the right people around me, particularly people whose roles involved taking responsibility and making decisions. Here, I knew the same to be true. From day one, I applied many of the life skills and lessons I had picked up. I learned on the job, but getting the right people around me was a real challenge – these managers were slippier than the fish in the Den River!

Fortunately, I had a fantastic ally in the shape of football club secretary Dr John Evans. John is as passionate as I am about football – possibly more so – and very well educated, able to learn, apply and later even create rules. He is respected and well connected in the game, and his skills knowledge and experience were assets that I valued very highly. If I needed help or advice in any new or sticky situation, and there were plenty of those – I knew I could rely on John.

It took us a short time to appoint a new manager - Roy Barry, the ex-Coventry defender who had been managing East Fife. We had just sold local youngster Kirk Stephens to Luton for £5,000, then a club record transfer fee. It was hard to let such a talented lad go, but I wanted the best for him, and no-one was more proud than I was when he went on to win an England semi-professional cap (now England "C").

Barry's reign began well; we won the Birmingham Senior Cup before preparing to set off for the Anglo-

Italian Tournament. I was delighted to be part of a very smart-looking Boro squad which went to Italy – I bought every player a smart blue blazer and had wonderful embroidered club badges sewn onto the breast pockets. People stared as we queued at Gatwick - I reckon they thought we were the England team. And, well, I may be a Paddy but we were representing England!

The Class of '78 – dressed to impress!

We lost 2-0 to Reggiana, then played out of our skins against Paganese, a side going for the Italian Third Division title. We won 3-1, ending the trip on a high.

Off the field, I again had to see off financial troubles. To pay an electricity bill, I had to sell a striker, Roger Jones. This was not well received by the fans, so the next time we needed to pay a big bill I decided to sell off a limited edition Queen's Silver Jubilee solid silver rose bowl I had bought. I could have raised money discreetly, but I saw an opportunity to raise awareness for the Boro's financial situation in the local press. My move triggered a big news story – *Chairman sells family silver to save club* - and kick-started an appeal that eventually raised nearly £15,000. Local hotelier Fred Kilpatrick, who bought the bowl, gave it back to me as a personal gift when I was struggling over fifteen years later.

So came to an end my first season as chairman. We had beaten a league side in the Cup before losing to a divot, we'd had four managers, played in Europe, and kept the wolves from the door. It was clear from the beginning that football was going to be a roller coaster ride!

It was certainly hard work, and I was never shy of putting in the hours, or rolling up my sleeves and getting stuck in with the manual work. I was having a fantastic time despite the financial pressures and juggling the needs of business and family.

But there's no doubt that my hobby had very quickly become an obsession.

During a hectic season we had found time to launch a lottery, in conjunction with Ladbrokes. Thanks to a lot of help from John Moore, we were the first non-league club to take what was then a revolutionary step. We opened a Boro Club Shop in the town, enlisted an army of ticket agents, and the lottery was a big success. In the first week we sold 39,000 tickets and made £4,000 profit. The money generated helped us pay for much-needed ground improvements, including a retainer wall at the back of the stand, new terracing and a car park. But before long, other clubs and the local council jumped on the bandwagon with lotteries of their own, and it became a very competitive space.

I quickly came to realise that I had inherited control of a company that was in a bad state, with poor records and systems. If I was going to run the company properly and achieve my ambitions for the club, I needed to know what was going on.

I gave my bookkeeper at CIP the job of maintaining the club's financial records, and I brought in CIP's lawyers, Coventry firm Varley Hibbs, to sort the administrative systems and reconstitute the company. They put in place regular board meetings, AGMs, annual returns and statutory accounts, a process for electing and re-electing directors, and correct and complete recording of any share transactions.

Beyond that I had bigger plans, to give the club facilities that would not be out of place in the Football League, to give the fans the comfort and atmosphere they deserved.

I unveiled plans for a £1 million super stadium at Manor Park, incorporating a state-of-the-art sports hall on vacant land next to the ground. Such a facility would enable the club to give something back to the community. But the council blocked the project, saying that transport, access and parking at the site, a mile from the town centre, was inadequate.

I reluctantly accepted the decision, and found land in Weddington, a mile and a half out of town, just off the A5. Visiting fans could reach the ground without having to pass through Nuneaton's town centre, without needing to navigate its infamous ring road, the "Roanne Ringway", which took traffic into, rather than around, the town (and still does!).

The new site had more than adequate space for parking; I covered every possible council objection. But the truth of the matter was that they saw the stadium and sports hall as a competitor for their own facilities, and saw no need for modern, comfortable or Football League-standard facilities for the town.

I was frustrated by their tunnel vision. How many towns in England had I only heard of because of their successful football team? How might the town of Nuneaton benefit by visits twenty times a year not from a couple of hundred travelling football supporters, but from many thousands?

Had my plans been successful, Nuneaton Borough would have been a pioneer, leading the trend that took off very shortly afterwards for clubs to rebuild or move their stadiums – these days many a professional club has done so.

Manor Park, in a prime location, was perfectly placed for residential use. Selling the ground at that time would have brought in £1 million to pay for the new stadium in its entirety. It was a no-brainer. But who am I? I'm only an uneducated Irishman…

I later learned that the council, and others with influence in the town, didn't want to see an uneducated Irishman raise the club's profile, or receive praise for a fantastic, revolutionary idea. So they put it about that I could only be doing it for personal gain. Nothing was further from the truth – I was prepared to give full financial disclosure, and all profits from the project would have been retained 100% for the benefit of the club and the town. But my plan was shot down.

Back on the pitch, FA Cup magic came again in November 1978, when Boro were involved in three tremendous games with Matlock. We drew 2-2 at home, 2-2 again at Matlock, and won a second replay, on neutral ground at Stafford, 2-1. This put us into the First Round Proper again, another home draw against a League side. But Crewe Alexandra beat us 2-0.

Roy Barry was doing a great job. He achieved our aim of finishing high enough in the Southern League to ensure a place in the brand new Alliance Premier League, which was to kick off the next season, and we finished the campaign showing a £15,000 profit.

A new dawn for Non-League Football

I have mentioned Club Secretary Dr JJ Evans. John was, and still is, an intelligent and passionate man who understands the administrative process of running a football club better than anyone I've met.

Such was John's reputation in the game that he was invited to sit on the committee that formed the

LITTLE FECKER!

Alliance Premier League. John was involved in writing its rules, and I donated the trophy that is presented to the League's winners.

As the APL was such a significant change to our national game, I have taken an opportunity and invited John to record for posterity the process of forming the APL. I am proud to reproduce his words here.

<u>Development of The Alliance Premier League 1974-1979</u>

The campaign for the setting up of what was originally referred to as the National League actually began in 1974, following a 'phone conversation between Jack Leighton, Chairman of Gateshead United, and myself, originally about a pre-season friendly! We agreed to argue for a new league and whilst he spoke to clubs in the Northern Premier League, I approached the best clubs in the south.

Fairly soon it became obvious that while the management committee of the NPL was largely in favour, their counterparts in the south were mostly against the idea. Meetings were held around the country, including one in Nuneaton in 1976. Support in the south grew gradually. This was the situation when Noel Kelly joined the board of NBFC in July 1976, and he became an enthusiastic supporter.

After he became Chairman in 1977, Noel continued to support the plan, accompanying me to meetings at various venues. In 1978, at their respective AGMs, the two leagues, North and South, agreed to set up the new competition for season 1979-80. We actually carried out a coup in the south that day, using the voting for management committee members as an opportunity to remove the anti-brigade and replace them with supporters of the scheme. I was one such who was elected!

The rules were settled by the spring of 1979, and approved at a meeting held at Highfield Road, Coventry, where the inaugural Management Committee was elected (again including me). The first AGM was held in Solihull on 2nd June 1979, and the new league kicked off in August of the same year.

Once the competition began, it needed a trophy to play for. Noel Kelly agreed to part-sponsor it and pay 25% towards the cost involved. League chairman Jim Thompson was to procure the actual trophy.

Typically, Noel showed far more enthusiasm than anyone else involved. He approached a designer, obtained approval for a really appropriate design for a league which stood at the peak of the semi-professional pyramid, and then paid for it in full.

This, as much as anything, reflected Noel's commitment to football in general and to NBFC in particular. This act of generosity, taken together with his known enthusiasm for the competition, led to his being elected as a Life Member of the APL in 1971. Sadly, at the time of writing he has never been invited to present his own trophy by the League itself, which even, for a few weeks in 2005, denied the extent of his involvement in the acquisition of the trophy.

Dr. John J Evans

LITTLE FECKER!

The Noel Kelly Trophy – presented to the winners of the Alliance Premier League (now the Football Conference)

To set ourselves up for 1979-80, the first season of the Alliance Premier League, we strengthened the squad. Barry bought striker Eamonn Pugh from Sutton for £4,000, and grabbed six players from Atherstone Town, who had gone bust. Unfortunately we lost the brilliant Trevor Peake, given his League break with a £15,000 transfer to Lincoln. Trevor went on to great things, at Coventry City and Luton Town.

We went out of the FA Cup to non-league Northwich Victoria in the First Round Proper, but things went much better in the FA Trophy, a realistic route to

Wembley. In February we beat Hyde 4-1 and Gainsborough 2-1 to reach the last 16.

In the next round we entertained Barnet. I arranged to have the match filmed, in colour and with a commentary. We won 2-1, and I occasionally get out the projector, pull the rolls of cine-film from the drawer and re-live the day. The scenes in the dressing room after the victory, the players being interviewed while getting changed, make amusing viewing!

The quarter-finals meant a tough trip to Dagenham. But the drama started before kick-off, with a midnight trans-Atlantic phone call, the night before the game.

Former Arsenal and Leicester star Jon Sammels was on loan to us from Canadian club Vancouver Whitecaps, and was proving a valuable member of the team. Vancouver had informed John Evans that they had placed Sammels into the general "pool" of US league players. This was a point in the American season rather like our modern transfer window where players could be sold, but with or without their permission. If no-one came in for Sammels – and he had made it clear that he would not be returning to America to play – then there would be no problem and he could play against Dagenham.

John Evans had spoken with Vancouver Chief Executive Les Wilson, and Les had been very helpful. But just before midnight on the night before the Dagenham game, Les called John at our London hotel to tell him that San Diego Sockers had claimed Sammels's registration at the very last minute.

LITTLE FECKER!

John Evans had to wake Jon Sammels and they phoned San Diego, who were happy for Sammels to play for Nuneaton. But without the release paperwork in place, Borough could be accused of fielding an ineligible player. The Sockers sent faxes to the US Soccer headquarters in New York, and to the FA in Lancaster Gate, clearing Jon to play for Nuneaton.

Early next morning, John Evans roused the FA's Competitions Manager Adrian Titcombe, whom we had made aware of the possibility of this scenario arising. Adrian agreed to travel from his home into central London to see if the paperwork had arrived. The fax from San Diego was there, but nothing from New York; the US Soccer staff had gone home for the weekend. There was nothing we could do.

This stunning news was conveyed to me on the morning of the game. It was the middle of the night in America - Sammels had to be ruled out. He was our main man in midfield and I knew his absence could mean the difference between victory and defeat.

More bad luck on the pitch: with Dagenham 2-1 up, the referee ignored a blatant goal-line handball. Instead of a penalty, which could have brought us, level, we went further behind. Mark Neale reduced the arrears but it was all over. A 3-2 defeat, the Wembley dream disappeared for another year.

The referee in the game was Cliff Maskell, a Football League referee. He waltzed into the boardroom after the game and was welcomed like a long lost brother, and handed a very large gin and tonic that had been poured for him in advance. I watched John Evans storm out of the boardroom in disgust – to this day the only time in over forty years that he has turned down hospitality as a visitor!

A bad day at the office: with son Sean and John Evans at Dagenham

On Monday morning the staff at US Soccer in New York found the fax from San Diego and immediately sent permission to the FA for Sammels to play for Nuneaton. If we had managed a draw in Dagenham, Jon could have played in the replay. It's a thin line between success and failure...

Just a week later Roy Barry was lured away to Oxford United and we made Graham Smith manager. But we managed a respectable finish in the Alliance and put two trophies - the Birmingham Senior Cup and Midland Floodlit Cup - in the cabinet.

My fourth season as chairman was a disaster. We went out of the FA Cup at the first hurdle, beaten 1-0 at Kidderminster after I had taken the players to a

LITTLE FECKER!

local hotel and got them in the mood by showing them film footage of our 1977 win against Oxford. It was to no avail - we turned in a mediocre display and from then on things went sour.

I learned an important lesson that day: match days are for the players and the manager. It's not the time for chairmen and directors to step in and take charge. The players weren't interested in watching an old match – I was wrong to show it to them.

Boro lost eight of the next nine games to slide down the table. Attendances dropped from 1,200 to less than 500. Smith resigned.

Sammels took temporary charge as we looked for a permanent replacement. A popular favourite with some Board Members was Jeff Blockley, the former Coventry and Leicester centre-half.

Colchester United had put in a bid of £30,000 for our centre-half, John Glover, and there was a belief that by appointing Blockley, who was prepared to play as well as manage, we would be able to take the cash from Colchester without weakening the team.

I went to see Jeff Blockley. We got on well, although we spent a lot of time talking about engineering rather than football. In any case, I had discovered that highly-respected Graham Carr was both available and keen to join us, so I made a quick approach.

Carr, a Geordie, had made his mark as a player and manager; he had been to Wembley with Telford and done well at Weymouth. He lived nearby in

Northampton, and within a couple of days was Nuneaton's new team boss.

It also turned out that Colchester could not really afford to take John Glover. All they could offer was £5,000 down and the rest in bits and drabs. Given that Graham was strongly opposed to the proposed transfer, and that the payment terms offered were so poor, we turned down the Essex club's approach, and John stayed at the club for several more years.

Carr's first test came in January 1981. After a 2-1 defeat at home to Ashington in the FA Trophy, he came out with a crushing statement: "The team is just not good enough."

He made two big signings: Trevor Morley for £7,700 and Richard Dixey for £9,500. I had paid for Morley out of my own cheque book, but it was too late, the miracle didn't come. At the end of the season we lost our Alliance place.

Proud alumni – Trevors Peake and Morley

But I could see Carr's ability and stood by him. He was a big success, staying at Manor Park for four years and fashioning what was in my opinion the best team the club had ever had.

But now Boro were back in the Southern League - and the great fear was that we might stay there. I made a decision: whatever the cost, we must bounce straight back. I proposed, and the board agreed, that instead of reducing wages, which is normal following relegation, the players should keep the same level of pay. Carr bought Barry Lowe from Worcester for £6,000, and former League players Tommy Robson and Roy Clayton.

Pre-season preparation was perfect. I decided we needed something different, something special, and treated the team to four days at Henlow Grange, a luxurious health farm deep in the Bedfordshire countryside. Carr and Sammels put the players through their paces at six o'clock every morning, and training sessions were followed by wax baths, massages, muscle-toning and even ballet lessons! The Henlow Grange management gave me a great deal but the trip still cost me a pretty penny – I didn't care; it did wonders for the players and for team spirit. When the season started, the lads were raring to go.

In the first 14 games Boro registered 10 wins. Carr was named Manager of the Month. We beat Tividale and Bromsgrove in the FA Cup. By Christmas we were looking and feeling invincible. We were on cloud nine. But then came the inevitable hiccup.

We were drawn away in the FA Cup to Bishop Auckland. The team stayed in Darlington overnight, and I arranged a British Rail 'special' for fans to travel 200 miles north by train.

We got to the ground early, only to receive a police message to say that the Boro train had broken down and our supporters were stranded. We could do nothing: the match kicked off with only a handful on the terraces behind our goal. Despite the lack of support we took a deserved early lead and all was going well. Then, after twenty minutes, a side gate burst open and over 600 Nuneaton fans poured onto the ground. They ran across the pitch to get to the away end. It was mayhem – after a nightmare trip they had centre stage and were venting their frustration. The game was held up and our players lost concentration. We crashed to a shock 4-1 defeat.

Being out of the major cup competitions left us able to focus on our priority - getting back into the Alliance. Bad weather forced a six-week break which cost us over £5,000 in lost revenue; I had to turn down an invitation to participate in the Anglo-Italian Tournament because we could not afford to travel.

In February 1982, with Boro top of the league and our closest neighbours Bedworth United in second place, the clubs met at Bedworth. The attendance was an astonishing 5,157, a league record and the highest league gate at Bedworth for many years. We lost 1-0, but then beat Redditch 5-0, destroyed title challengers Alvechurch 3-0 on their own ground, and a 1-0 home win over Bedford clinched the title.

LITTLE FECKER!

We had pulled it off. Signing tricky winger Robson, 37, was a master stroke by Carr. He and Sammels were ambassadors for the club on and off the field. The players listened and looked up to the experienced duo. Their attitude was first class, two of the finest footballers ever to wear a Nuneaton shirt. Robson finished the season as top scorer with 26 goals.

My First Boardroom Battle

In the four years since my arrival we had put the club back on its feet - things were going well on the pitch and now was a good time to secure our financial future. During the 1981-2 season we negotiated with Nuneaton Council to buy Manor Park, at a bargain price of £25,000. Owning the ground would give us freedom to further improve facilities, and we could start to earn revenues from selling advertising space.

The board met to discuss how we might raise £25,000, and I was confident of unanimous support for the move. But one board member, Alf Scattergood, who had been with the club since the 1960's, seemed dead set against us buying the ground.

He couldn't give a valid reason for his objection, he just kept saying "we don't need to own the ground". I disagreed, then pointed out the challenge: the Council would want the £25,000 in one lump sum, and the club would not be able to get a mortgage. It was clear that we were short of the necessary cash. Scattergood suddenly changed his tack, and got very interested in the deal. He started shouting. His face was like a beetroot and he got really awkward and stroppy.

He banged the table, and said: "I'll put in £10,000 to help buy the ground - but there will be conditions."

He wanted 10% interest on the loan. I pointed out that it was in the company's articles that directors could not take more than 7%, and even then only if the club was making a profit. Up to this time all loans put into Boro by anyone were made for the love of the club. I had already put significant amounts in, with no interest or conditions attached.

But Alf insisted on earning interest, and then demanded a further condition - that, in return for making the loan, he would be granted 51% of the shares – giving him control of the club. I said this was never going to happen. The meeting was adjourned, under a cloud of ill feeling.

I felt sick. I had thrown myself, heart, body and soul, into the football club, and this man thought he could oust me with a £10,000 loan! But I had learned an important lesson – since I was giving so much to the club, I needed to protect my position as chairman. Scattergood had shown me the way to do this – I needed to acquire a controlling shareholding.

I took legal advice, and approached a number of minority shareholders. Everyone I spoke to agreed to sell me some shares at face value. I pointed out that Scattergood might come and offer them double, but they all wanted me to be able to carry on my good work at the club. They said that in the event of a vote at an EGM or AGM, they would back me.

LITTLE FECKER!

All this politics and strategising was new to me, but I was heartened by the shareholders' response and went into the next meeting feeling confident. I had increased my shareholding, though the transfers still had to be verified by the board, and if ratified I would still be just shy of a majority shareholding. But at this stage I had not canvassed a single board member.

We started where we had finished the previous meeting. Alf's offer was still on the table. Then it was my turn to speak. I placed the share transfer forms on the table and said that if the board agreed to accept the transfers, I would make a further significant financial commitment to support the club. I took out two cheques, one for £12,500, an interest free loan to help to buy the ground, the other for £2,500, a gift to launch an appeal fund. I said it was their decision and I would leave them to make up their minds.

After fifteen minutes in the social club I returned – my offer had been accepted. Scattergood had sunk so far into his chair you could hardly see his face. The board had voted to keep me in charge as Chairman, and to accept my increased shareholding in the club. I had made no mention to this point of any intention or desire to acquire a *majority* shareholding.

It was noted at this point that the £12,500 cheque took my total loans in the club to around £40,000. Out of the blue, Alan Evans said that he thought that, having put so much money into the company, I should own a controlling interest. There was silence. I confirmed how many shares I had, and said it was entirely up to the board if anyone wanted to sell me some of their shares. Alan Evans immediately offered to sell me 10 of his. The other members voted to accept this, and as a result I now owned 50.35% of Nuneaton Borough Football Club.

Shortly after this Alf stepped down as a board member to become honorary President. Little did I realise that what had happened on this night was going to cost me dearly.

I believe that after his boardroom defeat, a germ of revenge began to fester in Scattergood's brain. It was probably the first time Alf had been beaten fairly and squarely in business.

I soon learned that the club's success under my chairmanship was getting under Alf's skin. In a casual chat with the steward of a local club where Alf was a regular, I learned that he was referring to me as "the fucking Irishman", and saying things like, "I don't know who he thinks he is" and "He's got no right to be running an English football club!"

I was shocked; I'd had my leg pulled about being Irish hundreds of times, but this was real racism.

In 1973 Scattergood had been chairman for a while but had failed. Having misjudged the mood of the fans, he sacked 28 year-old club manager David Pleat, who went on to great success as manager of Luton Town and Tottenham Hotspur. With fans shouting "Scatty Out!", Alf was forced into resignation.

Scattergood could now see that I was taking the Boro somewhere and would get the credit. But whether or not his comments against me were born out of jealousy, I was not happy with his vociferous and blatant racism.

But there was little or nothing I could do about it – I decided to focus on the job in hand. Things were progressing well; we completed the purchase of the ground. Alf still came to matches, and we were civil to one another in the boardroom and on the team coach. But I was concerned with the way Alf was behaving when he came to matches. He always loved a drink, but was having four or five large gins even before kick off. He became an embarrassment with the things he would say.

When I first joined the board, I was enthusiastic at matches and shouted support from the directors' box. One day Alf took me aside and said I should show more decorum. I was taken aback for a second but then thought perhaps he was right. Now I was telling him the same thing! He was out of order and, more importantly, affecting the club's reputation.

I often cringed with horror as Alf shouted obscenities at the ref or made stupid comments in the boardroom. At an important meeting in Coventry, Jim Thompson had been elected chairman of the new Alliance Premier League. I did not believe my ears when Alf warned him that Noel White - later chairman of Liverpool - was after his job. Thompson was aghast.

Though we were founder members of the Alliance and instrumental in non-league football's most important move, and though I had donated the trophy and been appointed a life member, Thompson always displayed a negative opinion of Nuneaton Borough. I can only put it down to Scattergood's inappropriate remark

Plan X

Purchase of Manor Park allowed me to reinvigorate a scheme I had previously announced in 1978. We referred to this as *Plan X*, an ambitious plan to sell Manor Park and use the proceeds to build a brand new super stadium on the outskirts of the town.

I had been approached by a developer who was interested in acquiring our ground. I put it to the board and they were all quite excited. Nothing could be settled at this stage but we realised it was something we had to consider, as a definite way forward for the good of the club.

At first I could never envisage watching Boro play anywhere other than Manor Park. I used to think about some of our staunch fans, such as Mrs Pagett, who had their own little spot where they stood for every home match. But, eventually, I began to think that Plan X could be the answer and the salvation of the club. I could see big advantages in us having a marvellous new ground, complete with ready-made stands, plenty of car parking, additional sports facilities and even conference rooms.

I also knew we never had any hope of progressing into the League if we stayed at Manor Park. The ground, adjacent to a canal, didn't have enough exits to enable larger crowds. Years ago, I even looked at the possibility of building a bridge out across the canal, but we were quoted £150,000.

The alternative was to sell the ground and use the proceeds to move to a new home. I actually had an offer on the table of £1.8million from a developer for Manor Park, on condition of planning consent. If the council had agreed to this, we could have given the town a £1million donation - and still had more than enough left to buy a new ground, build a new stadium and even buy a new team. I had first option on 17 acres on the outskirts of Nuneaton, which would have been an ideal site.

At the time the move would have been revolutionary, and since then many football clubs have done exactly that - and have not looked back.

Any profits made by a club through a developer have to be ploughed back into football. This is in the FA rules. In any case, all I was interested in was the future progress of Nuneaton Borough FC and in making sure we had suitable facilities ready for when we could stake a claim for a place in the Football League. This was my dream.

Back in the Alliance

Season 82-83 saw us back in the Alliance. Carr signed a young striker called Paul Culpin, and early evidence of his prowess came quickly, when he hit the net six times in a 9-0 Floodlit Cup win against Redditch. One of those six goals, a volley with the ball dropping over his shoulder as he raced forward, ranks among the best goals I have seen in my life, at any level.

We gained our revenge over Bishop Auckland, winning 3-1 in the FA Trophy with Culpin scoring twice. But we were feeling the pinch financially, after having to invest heavily to reclaim our Alliance status. The club was hit with a tax bill of £44,000 and I travelled to Downing Street with a personal plea to Maggie Thatcher for help. Our MP Les Huckfield also intervened to get us a stay of execution from the Inland Revenue.

Our FA Cup hopes were in shreds early on, when Oldbury scored a shock 2-1 win on our ground. I will always accept some responsibility for this - because of a remark I made to Graham Carr just before the game. He was sitting in the Vice Presidents' bar, watching television. In a good mood, I asked Graham, "What are Oldbury like?" He mumbled that he didn't know. I snapped, "What? Haven't you had them watched?" And I knew straight away that was the worse thing I could have asked. His face was like thunder. From that moment I think we had no chance of winning. I don't know what he said to the players in the dressing room before kick-off, but I'm sure my untimely criticism can't have helped. Instead of displaying his usual vociferous pitchside passion, Graham spent the whole game in the dug out in silence, as our team played like complete strangers.

This was a lesson I had to learn as a chairman: keep your manager in a happy frame of mind. I had hit a raw nerve by questioning the fact that Graham had not been to see Oldbury. He objected to me telling him how to do his job. It was as silly as that. An out-of-the-blue comment by me had put our manager's back up - and quite possibly cost us what could have been a money-spinning Cup run.

Fortunately, things went better in the league, and the team was really beginning to look good. By May we were serious contenders for the title. A 3,597 crowd saw a thrilling home clash against chief rivals Maidstone. It ended 2-2, with Trevor Morley missing a glorious chance of netting a last-gasp winner.

The result proved decisive. Our last fixture was on a Friday night at Runcorn. We won 1-0. But, the following day, Maidstone beat a below-strength Telford 6-0 to take the championship by one point.

A new points system was introduced by the Football League for the 83-84 season, with three points for a win and one for a draw. Wishing to be different, the Alliance management committee introduced two points for a home win and three for winning away. Seeing no reason to be inconsistent, I was against the idea, and even more so when the system cost us the championship. We finished the season in second, position. Had the Football League system been in place, we would have been champions

Vincie

You'll be thinking that football was the only thing on my mind, and in many ways it was. But I was still running CIP full time and seeing friends and family.

In September 1984, Joan and I celebrated our silver wedding anniversary with a big party in a marquee in the garden at Lutterworth Road. Vincie had enjoyed the party but the following week, at work he came into the office with his blue Crombie coat and said he wasn't feeling well. I told him to go home and get some rest. He lived not far from the office, just a ten-minute walk, so I was surprised to pass him as I was driving up his road on my way home. As I passed him he waved and looked ok, I guessed he'd perhaps popped into the bookies. When I got home twenty minutes later the phone rang. It was Dermot, Vincie's son. He just said "me dad's dead".

Vincie had had heart bypass surgery twice and a valve fitted 10 years before, and they never checked it again. He had not only survived but thrived, Vincie never wanted to go to a doctor, he never complained about anything and just got on with his work.

Vincie was one of the nicest blokes you could ever wish to meet, loved by everyone. I always felt privileged, not only to live and work with him, but to have him as my brother. His passing affected me badly, it seemed so unfair to lose such a close friend so young.

Life would get difficult for me a couple of years down the line, but loss of loved ones is different, a deeper pain then anything I ever suffered.

God bless you, Vincie.

LITTLE FECKER!

1984-5 – Second again!

At the beginning of 84-85, Paul Richardson, midfield tiger, was sold to Derby for £15,000 and Eddie McGoldrick joined from Kettering for £1,000. This, another astute signing by Carr, was the final piece in the jigsaw, completing what is still considered Boro's best-ever team. It contained no less than six players who were to go on to play in the Football League, including four who were to appear in the First Division (now the Premier League).

We had developed Timmy Smithers from a youngster after spotting him at a Coventry Alliance club. He went to Oxford. Richard Hill (Northampton, Oxford, Watford), Eddie McGoldrick (Northampton, Crystal Palace, Arsenal, Eire World Cup 1994), Trevor Morley (Northampton, Manchester City, West Ham, Reading), Paul Culpin (Coventry, Northampton, Peterborough), Stuart Hamill (Scarborough) and Frank Murphy (Barnet), Brendan Phillips, Willie Gibson and Everton Carr all tasted League experience, and Richard Dixey and Ian Bennyworth, two big strong defenders who were definitely League material. It really was one hell of a side.

It was also a very exciting one to watch. And, with a bit more luck, we could have swept all before us that season. As it was, we had to be content with runners-up in the league, for the second successive year, and a defeat in the First Round of the Cup, in an away replay, after extra time. That was at Scunthorpe - who had brought the impressive cricketing legend Ian Botham to Nuneaton.

With Boro high in the table, Graham Carr was offered the manager's post at Northampton Town, and I couldn't blame Graham for accepting. We'd had an up-and-down relationship but respected each other – he had done a great job and brought amazing players to the club. Graham had League ambitions and went with my best wishes. He later achieved national recognition when his Northampton team knocked Coventry City out of the FA Cup, and is now the very highly respected Chief Scout at Newcastle United, responsible for their 'French Revolution'. Graham's son is the hugely popular comedian Alan Carr.

The Dream Team: Graham Carr's Future Stars

Richard Dixey was appointed caretaker boss to see out the season, and had the distinction of winning the April Manager of the Month award with three wins out of three, as we finished second again, behind Wealdstone at the top of the league.

LITTLE FECKER!

Near the end of the season came the awful fire at Bradford, turning a spotlight on ground safety throughout the country and, for me, our old wooden main stand.

New manager Peter Morris had played at Ipswich and Norwich and had gained managerial experience with Peterborough, Mansfield, Crewe and Southend. Culpin was sold to Coventry in a £50,000 deal, Morley and Hill went to Northampton for £30,000 and we collected a £3,800 bonus for being runners up and second highest goal scorers in the league.

Incredibly, the points system which had thwarted us twelve months earlier did so again. Under the Football League system, we would have been champions - again!

In 1985-86 Enfield won the league clearly, under whichever system was favoured, and at that point the experiment which had cost us so dear was abandoned, and the Alliance reverted to the League's points system.

My ninth season as chairman saw Boro again reach the First Round of the FA Cup to entertain a League club, former Cup finalists Burnley. But I had already decided that Morris had to go. We had done well in the Cup, but were struggling in the league, with 10 defeats in 14 games. Morris departed and Dixey again took over in a caretaker role.

The Burnley tie was exciting. Boro trailed 2-0 but fought back to 2-2, only for Burnley to grab victory in the last minute, goal scored by Warwick Rimmer, at that time the oldest professional player in the League!

A week later popular Irishman Jimmy Holmes, became Boro's new manager. Jimmy was the Republic of Ireland's youngest full international when he was 17, and played at the top level with Coventry and Spurs. He had been coaching at Peterborough but lived in Coventry and agreed to combine managerial duties with playing. His main job was to salvage our league position. A 1-1 draw at Telford in May kept Boro up on goal difference.

So we swung into 1986-87 - Boro reached the FA Cup First Round for the seventeenth time ever - seven of which were under my chairmanship - but Rochdale dealt us a 3-0 defeat. I drowned my sorrows with Rochdale director, entertainer Tommy Cannon.

McGoldrick went to Northampton for £15,000 - as our balance sheet was "leaked" to the Tribune to reveal a club heavily in debt.

As I celebrated my 50th birthday with friends and family at a party at home, I ran through the highs and lows of a fascinating ten years since that snowy day in Lincoln in 1976.

But events were already in process that were to ensure this would be my last season as Chairman of Nuneaton Borough.

Fun Times at Manor Park

I hope I've given you a brief taste of the harder side of running a football club – the disappointments and frustrations on and off the field. I'll warn you now – these were nothing compared with what was to follow. In my second book, *Dirty Feckers*, I'll tell you all about what happens when a jovial and honest Irishman finds himself in the claws of greedy, powerful men.

But first, I want to share with you the fun times, the highlights of my ten years in charge, both on and off the pitch. Here is just a small selection of fun stories.

Sights for Sore Eyes

At a home game, our 'keeper took a knock which dislodged both contact lenses. The game stopped while a dozen players, the referee and linesmen crawled around the penalty area – the rest standing around its edge as if waiting for a penalty to be taken – or perhaps to stop the lenses from escaping. It was quite a sight from the stand. After a good five minutes the keeper sidled up to the referee, bent and coughed to get his attention, and whispered something in his ear. The game resumed immediately – I was worried that our keeper had decided to play on with blurred vision, but he played well and conceded no goals. After the game, I asked the 'keeper what he'd said to the ref. He replied' "I told him, 'Sorry ref, they'd just slid down off my eyelids!'"

On another occasion, centre back John Glover lost a contact lens in the penalty area with only five minutes of the game gone. After holding up the game for a couple of minutes John, ever the gentleman, said "don't worry ref, I can play with one eye". After the game John went back out onto the pitch and found the lens within 30 seconds!

During one game at Manor Park with 20 minutes left, fog blew in off the canal, and half the pitch was swathed in dense fog. The referee had no option but to call off the game. The lads showered and were dressing to go to the bar when someone said "Where's Bob?" Bob Knight, our keeper, was still keeping guard between his posts, worried that he hadn't seen or heard his defenders for a while, but concerned that if he went looking for them he might get caught on the break!

On the Road

Getting to a game on time was often a challenge, and if we were late we were fined. On one occasion the bus ran out of diesel, on another a substitute driver pulled onto the hard shoulder to have his regulation tea break, and on a third we were fined after being delayed by a motorway accident in which several people had been killed.

But Bill George, our regular bus driver, was a consistent source of laughs. On one occasion he had bought a brand new coach. As we were heading up the M1 to a game it started to rain heavily. Bill started flicking switches on the huge console, and it became obvious that he didn't have a clue where the switch for the wipers was. As the view out the front disappeared completely behind raindrops, Bill flicked switches faster and faster, and his face getting redder and redder. Eventually he conceded.

"Fuck it!" he yelled and ran his right forearm down the entire bank of switches. The windscreen wipers suddenly kicked in at full speed, the hazard lights began to flash, and the doors flew open!

The lads weren't going to let Bill forget this, and next time we played away they got on the bus one at a time, twenty seconds apart, and each asked him to show them that he knew where the wiper switch was before they'd take their seat!

After another away game the team was waiting for Bill to turn the bus round, so I got in and executed a perfect three point turn, though I have to admit it was scary, especially as the roguish players were encouraging me to believe that I had more space to manoeuvre than I really did – nothing would have made them laugh more than if the Chairman had pranged the new team coach! When Bill appeared, we were all sitting calmly – perhaps too calmly - in our places ready for the journey home. Well, Bill went loopy, demanding to know which of the players had dared to drive his precious bus. When no-one owned up he said, "Then you can all get off and walk!" I said "What do you mean Bill? It was facing this way when we came out". The players kept schtum – who was going to shop the man who paid the wages? Bill leaned over and whispered in my ear, "Noel, I want to know which of these cheeky feckers turned my bus round!" His eyes were blazing, and he was a big lad – I decided to stick with my story. "No-one drove your bus!" I insisted. Then Bill said, so why are we facing the wrong way down a ONE WAY STREET? The lads, the manager and trainer were in hysterics all around me. I couldn't keep a straight face, so I had to own up. Bill drove home in a bad mood, not sure whether to be annoyed at the Chairman for driving his bus, or the players for covering up for me!

Bill George not only drove our team bus, he owned the coach company (either he saw looking after the Boro as a perk, or he was short staffed and tight-fisted!). So he would turn up at games in his expensive Crombie coat, and more often than not he'd follow the directors into the boardroom. After a game at Kettering, Bill was in the boardroom nursing a large glass of whisky, and a Kettering director whispered to me, "Your new director can sure knock the whisky back – I hope he's not driving when you get back!" I replied, "Ooh, he'll be driving sooner than that!"

Directors at Maidstone were less hospitable. When they discovered that Bill wasn't a director they asked him to leave the boardroom and drink in the Vice President's bar. Bill looked down his nose at the Maidstone Chairman, downed his whisky, wandered over to the drinks cabinet, poured himself a VERY large one, and wandered off to drink it in the bar!

LITTLE FECKER!

Richard Hill, tough nut!

The coach back to Nuneaton after an away game was only one leg of the journey. It would drop players at pre-arranged points, from which they would be collected if they'd been drinking, or drive themselves home if they hadn't.

One evening on our way home from a match, we had dropped six players off at Leicester Forest East service station, and the coach set off back to Nuneaton. It was after midnight, and a little misty, but the roads were quiet. As we entered the roundabout to take us onto the M69, we saw two cars on the roundabout that had obviously been in a head-on collision. A couple of people were wandering aimlessly around – we appeared to be first on the scene.

I asked the driver to stop the bus and got off to check that everyone was ok . I called to the two men, who on seeing me panicked, screamed at each other in a foreign language, got into a car – which was facing the wrong way – and drove off – the wrong way round the large roundabout. As I wandered over to the remaining car I could see that it was empty.

Then someone shouted from the bus "Hey, that's Richard Hill's car!" And indeed it was, though there was no sign of our midfielder. Three of us pushed the car out of harm's way while five or six of the lads wandered around shouting for Richard, in case he was lying injured or wandering around dazed – his windscreen was cracked and it was clear that he'd head-butted it from the inside.

Once we were clear that Richard wasn't around, we got back on the coach and headed back to Nuneaton. At Manor Park I jumped straight into my car and headed round to Richard's house – his front door was wide open, and he was sitting by the fire with a large glass of whisky, shaking and obviously in shock.

Richard was okay – the numbskulls had come the wrong way round the roundabout and when Richard swerved to avoid them they had swerved the same way and managed a perfect head-on collision. I asked him how he'd got home.

"Oh, the next car to come round the roundabout was one of the lads. He saw me chasing these two twats up and down the road, I was ready to kill them! He threw me in his car and brought me home!"

Graham Carr's car

I once did Graham Carr a favour by selling his car to a friend of mine. Unfortunately, the friend took the car but was slow in paying for it. This was upsetting Graham and I was firmly in the middle – not a good situation when you're trying to run a happy club!

The night before a game Graham was staying in a Nuneaton hotel, so I drew £300 out of my bank account and took it down to the hotel to give to him. I expected to find him in the bar, but was told that he was in his room, having gone to bed early.

"I wouldn't disturb him, he's in a foul mood and specifically said he didn't want to see you!"

LITTLE FECKER!

Undeterred, I went up, to find Graham pacing his room in his pyjamas and dressing gown, fuming over not having been paid for his car. Seeing no point in trying to talk sense into him, I dropped the £300 on the bed and went back to the bar.

I ordered a drink, and before I could pay for, it a hand holding a ten pound note appeared over my shoulder. "I'll get that." It was Graham, in club blazer, slacks and collar and tie. Graham was always capable of pulling off a surprise, but I have often wondered how he dressed so quickly!

Looking after our Visitors: boardroom etiquette

Richard Hill was a character. After a home game he wandered into the boardroom – out of bounds to players – where we were entertaining visiting directors. Cool as a cucumber, he waltzed over to the buffet table, pick up a salmon sandwich and took a huge bite. With his mouth full, he shouted "Hey everybody, these are better than the fucking players get!" And with that he picked up four sandwiches in each hand and strode out of the room! We'd won, so I was in too good a mood to get mad with him, but the visiting directors were stunned!

On another occasion, I noticed soggy wet salad sandwiches in the boardroom buffet. I was embarrassed, the visitors were eyeing the sandwiches warily. "Who on earth made these?" I asked a fellow director, "we'll have to sack them!" He replied, "Actually, it was my missus!"

I treated every home game like a wedding. I was greeting honoured guests, and was keen to feed them well, ply them with drink and generally impress – I wanted everyone in the league to spread the word that Manor Park was an excellent place to visit. I was disciplined, thorough and well prepared; things generally went well.

However, on one occasion I was doing my usual pre-match inspection, when I checked the toilets used by visiting directors. Proudly occupying the bowl was the largest stool I've ever seen (and believe me I've seen many!). I flushed the loo, knowing that this was a pointless effort.

Behind me, I heard the door bang and someone shout "Noel, our visitors are here!" Lacking a big bucket to wash away the enemy, I phoned the office manager from the boardroom. "There's a problem in the VP's toilet, can you please sort it?"

As I went out to greet our guests, I saw the office manager run into the loo… with a big pair of scissors!

I bought him a well-earned pint that evening, and he assured me that the scissors were in the bin…

Unwelcome guests

Thieves broke into the club office one night, cutting through a partition wall and into the back of the safe. The fact that there was nothing in the safe must have irritated them – it was huge, standing almost five feet high – it must have taken them forever to cut the entire back off with an acetylene torch. If they'd gone round the front of it, they'd have found that it wasn't even locked! Another night a bunch of thieves broke into the social club bar and sat and got pissed - the police turned up and just arrested them.

Socialising with Nuneaton star Larry Grayson

Bonfire burgers

During my time at Nuneaton I was proud to throw a lavish bonfire party every November. I was always a bit of a pyromaniac, and it was great to light a big fire and lay on an impressive firework display on disused land next to the pitch. The events were great money-spinners for the club too.

In the lead up to one such occasion, a member of the social committee told me he could get decent sausages and beefburgers at half the price we usually paid. Delighted with the significant saving, I gave him the money for over 2,000 burgers and sausages. On the night, the bonfire was burning, the fireworks were fizzing, and the charcoal in the "Boro Fryer" was glowing hot. But there wasn't a piece of meat anywhere on the ground.

With a long queue of hungry revellers starting to get restless, the committee member arrived with the goods. I had been called over to appease the growing crowd, so I grabbed a plastic bag of sausages off the top of the pile, ripped it open and threw about a hundred onto the huge griddle. The sausages, no bigger than chipolatas, disappeared through the grille like lemmings over a cliff, straight into the fire.

Not to be fazed, I sent someone off to look for some foil trays while I opened the burgers. They were a bit thin, but at least they were big enough to sit on the grille. Well, at least until they got warm, when they melted like ice cream and joined the sausages in the flames.

The gathered crowd, thinking that this was part of the entertainment, cheered loudly and waited for me to produce the "real" food. I could do no more than apologise and tell them they could get a pie and chips around the corner later. I didn't recover the cost of the meat (the committee member's "butcher" friend said our coals must have been too hot), so had to write the evening off to experience.

Running a high profile bonfire had a downside; one year we went home to find the house had been burgled. Well, the whole town knew where we were.

LITTLE FECKER!

Our dog, a German Shepherd, was locked in a bedroom with the radio playing loud, to protect him from the sound of fireworks. The following year I arranged a housesitter!

Counting his chickens

In 1985 we hosted an FA Sunday Cup final at Manor Park, between Hobbies United from Norfolk, and Avenue FC from Birkenhead. The game was great, and brought in quite a crowd. I sat next to the Avenue chairman, whose team was winning 2-0 with minutes to go. "Do you have any champagne?" he asked. I said we had some in the fridge. "Can I give you £50 for a bottle?" Of course I said yes, and the bottle was on ice in a silver bucket on the boardroom table when we went down at full time.

Unfortunately, it was a case of counted chickens, as Hobbies rallied late and the game ended 2-2. The Avenue chairman said "Oh Noel, you're too kind!" He opened the champagne and celebrated like a winner, then scarpered. I never saw the £50. Avenue lost the tie in a second replay, so I suppose some sort of justice was done!

The Boro in Europe!

In March 1979 we headed to Europe for Boro's second excursion in the Anglo-Italian tournament. A highlight of the trip was a game against Paganese, in front of 13,000 excited fans, and televised across Italy. I wished the team good luck and went out to take a seat among the crowd – everyone sat on the concrete steps of the stadium. The two teams were lined up ready to shake hands, and quite a crowd was gathering on the pitch for what looked like an opening ceremony.

Suddenly a loud announcement came over the tannoy – El Presidente Nuneaton! El Presidente, Nuneaton! I looked around, wondering what was happening, and saw our trainer Dave Looms waving like a madman. He shouted up from the pitch "Noel, they want YOU!" I scurried down the steps, under the stand and out on the pitch. The noise was terrific, the crowd all rose and cheered. This is what it must be like to be famous, bloody hell!

I was introduced to the Paganese President. He presented me with three beautiful trophies, one for my Captain, one for our club, and a third, to take home to present to the officials of our town. I was taken aback by their hospitality and generosity, not least because I had nothing to give to them in return!

Our captain nudged me in the back and handed me a 6 inch cotton Nuneaton Borough FC pendant - the entire crowd must have seen him do it. As I handed it to the Paganese president the crowd went wild again – but boy was I embarrassed!

Anglo-Italian Toastie Recordbreaker!

For many years my love of food has been there for all to see, mainly around my waist. Perhaps there's something about the game of football, but during my

LITTLE FECKER!

reign as Chairman of Nuneaton I seemed to attract a number of rather large gentlemen to join me as co-directors, such that I was, if anything, regarded as a 'lightweight' among them. In fact the running gag for quite some time was, "What has eight legs and weighs 100 stones?" The answer being "The Nuneaton Borough board of directors!"

So imagine this little scene in Italy – the NBFC board enjoying a beer and a bite to eat. I have always liked my food, but have never been one to indulge to extremes. I am, however, particularly partial to a good toasted cheese sandwich. On the afternoon in question we were sitting in a hotel bar, and a large oval platter full of toasted sandwiches – cheese and ham, cheese and pickle, had arrived. And they were absolutely wonderful.

The hotel owner had spotted our 100-stone board, and obviously saw a revenue opportunity, so the first platter was swiftly followed by another. Then another. We were having a few beers and a laugh, and we just carried on eating the toasties. As I whipped the last toastie off what I thought had been the third platter, physio Dave Looms, slimmest member of our gathering, (excluded from the 100 stone tally) leaned over to me.

"Noel" he whispered, "You know you're the only one still eating." "Don't be daft!" I retorted, looking over at Messrs George, Hammond and Kay, the giants of our group. Bill George, the coach driver, was asleep, but Ted and Don were wide awake. Both were sitting as if in defeat, staring at me with amazement.

"What?" I asked. Dave pushed his clipboard in front of my face. He had a sheet of paper with five columns, one for each of us, and a series of tally marks. He had been keeping score.

Dave himself had eaten five toasted sandwiches (he said he would have stopped after three but it seemed impolite given the appetite shown by the rest of us). Ted Kay and Bill George had each eaten 12 toasties, and big Don Hammond had wolfed 20. I smiled at Don, very impressed. Then Dave moved aside the sheet of paper covering my column - the tally next to my name was a staggering 35.

I nudged Dave, "good joke!" Dave looked into my eyes - he was and has always been an honest man. "Excusi?" he called to the bar's owner, "How many sandwiches have we had?" Our host checked his pad and came over, apologetic. "Seven plates, Signor... 84 sandwich".

Dave threw his scoresheet onto the table – he had accounted for every last one. "Very sorry" said our host. "Sorry?" I asked. "Yes, would bring more, but no more bread!"

We thanked him and said that we wouldn't be needing more – to be told that I'd eaten 35 sandwiches I was suddenly feeling very full! After a couple of brandies we rose to leave, and the owner rushed to get the door. As I left he handed me a bottle of grappa with his compliments. "World Record!" he beamed.

LITTLE FECKER!

We were in Italy again in 1980, and at the time, the TV show Mork and Mindy was all the rage. One evening Roy Barry and I wandered down to the funfair, taking with us a holdall full of Nuneaton Borough paper hats, printed specially for the trip. As I handed one to the first young Italian lad I saw, he thanked me in Italian. Not understanding what he'd said (languages, including English, aren't my strong point!), I simply replied "Na-nu Na-nu!", Robin Williams style.

Within seconds, dozens of Italians were queuing up for our hats, screaming "Na-nu Na-nu!" at the top of their voices. We soon gave away the 250 hats, and for the rest of the evening, and on many occasions over the following few days, random youngsters would run up to us screaming "Na-nu Na-nu!"

At the end of our Anglo-Italian tour we were late leaving for the airport, and traffic was horrendous. Our coach driver had spent an age just trying to get out of the hotel into the packed street, and I'd had enough. I jumped out of my seat and marched out into the lunatic traffic, holding out my hand like a traffic cop to find us a way out.

The car I'd stepped in front of was a big silver Mercedes limousine, with blacked-out windows. I smiled by best cheeky Irish smile, but to be honest I think I was so worried that we'd miss our flight that my usual charm was perhaps not in evidence.

As the bus eased into the traffic the Mercedes nudged forward, bumping my legs. Any charm I was showing was knocked away with each nudge, and after the third I kicked the bumper of the Merc and moved to get back onto the coach.

The Merc shot forward and a rear window slid open. I saw an expensively dressed slim man on the back seat, then a gorilla-like arm shot out of the window and his bodyguard grabbed my tie.

I was nose to nose with one of the toughest men I've ever seen. "English?" he grunted. "Irish" I croaked. "You are lucky to be alive" he said, and as I looked into his eyes I knew he was telling the absolute truth. Before I could think of anything to say, something that would doubtless have landed me in deeper trouble, he smiled and pushed me away.

When we got to the airport there were scenes of mayhem in the departure lounge, and Dave Looms pointed to the information boards. "Our flight is cancelled". I was feeling close to panic as I approached the pretty young stewardess and asked for details. It had been a long trip, I was still recovering from my run-in with the mafia Mercedes, and I wanted to go home.

I explained that there were 23 in our party and we needed to get back, as we were a serious football team with an important fixture to get to. (It was, of course, our summer break, but she wasn't to know). I produced from my suitcase handfuls of Nuneaton Borough club pennants, photographs and para-phernalia. A crowd of airport staff gathered, and I showed them the lovely gifts we'd received from the Italian clubs we'd played, pennants, trophies, ornate decanters and sculptures. This convinced them that we were VIP guests, and initiated a flurry of activity, phone calls and girls waving clipboards. Within ten minutes thy told us they had "found" 23 seats on a flight to England. Ah, celebrity!

Weight!

Looking back at pictures from my youth, particularly when I was boxing in the army, I was quite a skinny young man. Hardly surprising given the general shortage of food in my childhood days in Ireland!

But I've battled with my weight for years. At my "peak", I weighed over 17 stones, and had a 48-inch chest – not bad for a man with a 27-inch inside leg!

I suppose I started to live the "good life" in the 1970's, as I built a successful business. Part of my approach to growing Coventry Industrial Pipework was that I always felt it important to entertain my best clients. I wanted to show them that by working with Noel Kelly they would not only get a fantastic engineering job, but also they would get to have some fun! Engineering can be a dry, serious business, and engineers aren't renowned for their sense of humour. It was clear from the start that when I took a client out, it was a release for them from the daily grind.

Almost without exception, entertaining a client meant high quality food, and lots of it. I had a number of favourite restaurants in Coventry – the Royal Court, Lino's and Quo Vadis among them. At one point I was eating at the Royal Court twice or three times a week, and bear in mind that this was just lunch – I was going home to Joan's big dinners every evening!

The dessert trolley at the Royal Court was to die for – both in terms of quality and choice. Even though there were rarely more than two or three days between my Royal Court visits, on most occasions I would find it impossible to choose just one dessert. The waitresses, of course, were keen to look after me!

"A bit of this and a bit of that, Mr Kelly?" "Why not?" was my enthusiastic response.

The waitresses were fantastic, professional and friendly, and the manageress, a lovely lady called Mary Spencer, would be close at hand to make sure every aspect of the meal was perfect. One day she popped her head over my shoulder, and said, "You know, one day you might try half that amount of gateau… and by itself!"

I was solid and fit, and hadn't noticed the pounds creeping up on me. My business-building success, hadn't gone to my head. But it had certainly gone to my waist, and to my stomach, my legs, my shoulders, my arms and my arse!

For the first time, I could see the excess weight in the mirror, and Mary's words hit me hard. I knew she was thinking of me, not the restaurant's profit margins. I had to do something, and fast.

I asked a client, who liked his food and drink as much as I did, how he kept in shape. "Easy," – he said, "I go to a health farm."

Less than a week after Mary's helpful input, I was lying on a massage table at Henlow Grange. "We get a lot of Irishmen in here," said the manager. "Young men like you, who work hard and play hard." He added, in a very matter-of-fact tone, "We save lives."

After so many scrapes with death as a child, I can confidently say that being able to afford to go to Henlow Grange saved my life as an adult. On my first visit, I took sorting myself out very seriously indeed. Isolated from the bad influences in my daily life, my conduct at Henlow was quite extreme, and it's not something I would recommend. But it worked for me. For a week, I ate hardly any food, drank no alcohol at all, and actually got some exercise! I did a bit of gardening at home, but all of a sudden I was walking, running, cycling, swimming and rowing. The adrenalin rush was fantastic, and I felt like I was back in the army, a fit young twenty year old!

I think the exercise jump-started my metabolism; the effects on my body were startling. I lost fifteen and a half pounds in six days, and I'd never felt so well!

When I got home, Joan was in for a shock. First, she could fit both her arms, up to her elbows, down the gap between me and the waistband of my suit trousers! And second, she had prepared my favourite Saturday lunch – fillet steak and fried eggs – but I could only eat a quarter of it!

I became a regular visitor to Henlow, and I met many celebrities. I was delighted to spend a week in the company of singer Barbara Dickson, who was on the

Two Ronnies BBC TV show on Saturday nights – with an audience of 20 million people! She was lovely, and sent me two tickets for her show when she came to Coventry on tour the following year.

As a boxer in the army and lifelong boxing fan, it was a great buzz to train with Barry McGuigan, who was on this way to becoming world featherweight boxing champion. Barry weighed in at just nine stones, but we were the same height and I reckoned his speed and experience would more than compensate for my 'slight' seven stone weight advantage. Yet he turned down my offer of a sparring session!

With Barry McGuigan at Henlow Grange

LITTLE FECKER!

We had a great few days, and he kept in touch. Three years later, on the night he beat Manuel Pedrosa to win his world title in 1985, I was at a football dinner in London. I got a call from Barry's management, inviting me to the after-fight party. It was 2am and Joan was ready for bed, so I dragged my son Sean away from the dance floor and we jumped in a taxi.

The cab couldn't get near the hotel entrance – the street was filled with celebrating McGuigan fans – but we were waved to the front of the huge throng and ushered into a packed hall, where we drank Guinness and Tuborg Gold, and sang Irish songs, including my favourite – Danny Boy - with Barry's dad Pat and about a thousand delirious Irishmen until 6am!

I was so pleased when Barry went on to win Sports Personality of the Year – he was, and is, a super man, an ambassador for his sport and a force of energy and unification for Ireland, north and south of the border. I am so proud to number him among my friends.

I was also lucky to meet footballer Malcolm McDonald, the wonderful actress June Whitfield, and the cast of Z-Cars, who were great fun! But my "Henlow Highlight" came in 1983. I got a call from boss Steve Peugeot. "Are you coming to see us any time soon, Noel?" "Of course!" I replied.

"Great! Well... how are you fixed... next week?" It seemed an odd suggestion. Then Steve explained - filming was soon to begin at Pinewood Studios of the big James Bond movie – Octopussy, and three of the "Bond Girls" were booked into Henlow for pre-shoot rest, relaxation and toning! I have to say that the photo, posed with them all surrounding me, is one of my favourites!

Luck of the Irish!

* * *

At the end of the 1980-81 football season, Nuneaton Borough had been relegated from the Conference. Now a lot of people in football, fans and professionals alike, say "relegation will do us good – we'll bounce straight back, and benefit from the experience." But many teams, good teams with a solid fan base and strong behind-the-scenes set up - drop and sink like a stone. This has been proven recently; my beloved "second team", Coventry City, after 34 uninterrupted years in football's top flight, have been on a one-way – downward – trip since relegation in 2001.

So, I was under no illusions about the task ahead. I felt the players needed the best possible start if they were going to leap straight back into the league we belonged in. In August 1981, John Evans organised a pre-season friendly match at Hitchin, and I arranged and paid for the whole team to spend a weekend at Henlow Grange.

As you've read, we took the season by storm. Graham Carr hugged me as we celebrated our title win in May 1982 and said "Boss, you gave us the best possible start to a season!" That's what Henlow can do.

Once, at Henlow, I thought my chance of celebrity had arrived. I was lying on a massage bed next to a reporter, who told me he was there to write about the Henlow experience. We had a great chat, I told him a bit about myself and then started telling jokes – I had him in stitches.

When his article appeared in the magazine he sent me a complimentary copy, and I have to admit I was quite excited as I opened it – what wonderful things had he said about my weight loss achievements? Which of my best jokes had he included? I'd convinced myself that the article would be as much about me as about the health farm.

Of course, I was wrong. I was mentioned, though. Briefly. The article began: "I'm lying on a massage bed, next to a bull-necked Irish pipe-fitter". *"Bull-necked"*? I'd lost a stone! *"Pipe-fitter"*? I was a company director, thank you very much, with my own business employing a dozen pipe-fitters and thirty others!

Despite my initial irritation, the reporter's 'journalistic licence' was harmless This was my first experience of how the press can manipulate fact to suit a purpose. I was to face sterner treatment in the years to come!

A director's diet

My eating habits were not restricted to trips overseas. One Monday I went to my doctor in Nuneaton with stomach pains, and he asked what I'd been eating.

"Nothing out of the ordinary" I replied. He asked me to list what I'd eaten – and drunk – over the weekend.

Well, Saturday had been an away game, so the list went a bit like this:

7.30am	Midland Rd Café, match day breakfast - bacon egg & sausage on toast. Coffee.
11.00am	M1 services: 2 hot sausage rolls. Coffee.
12 noon	Hotel near ground: couple of pre-lunch pints
1.00pm	Hotel – match day lunch – steak, chips & grilled tomato. Another pint.
2.00pm	Host's boardroom – pre-match drinks – two pints and a large scotch.
3.45pm	Boardroom half time: tea and cake. Ok, cakes
4.45pm	Boardroom (we like this boardroom) – post-match buffet: soup, sandwiches, quiche, vol-au-vents. Whisky (free whisky, large measures... who knows how much really?)

LITTLE FECKER!

- 5.30pm Host's social club – post-match drinks with the team – two (three?) pints…
- 8.00pm Fish & Chip shop, outskirts of Nuneaton – usually fish, but I was hungry, so steak & kidney pie, and chips.
- 9.30pm NBFC Social Club, the home straight – 2 quick pints to help the pie and chips down
- 11.00pm George Eliot Hotel – nightcap - several large malt whiskeys and a plateful of sandwiches (courtesy of the landlord's wife: very Irish, very insistent)

The doctor had long since stopped taking notes, and had called for a nurse, who appeared, wielding a length of rubber tube. As I finished the list, the doctor said "Drop your pants, lie on your side…"

The rumours are true! Ned likes a drink!

My second – and last - enema was every bit as unpleasant as the first, back in my days at the Sterling Metals. I became very wary about what I ate – oh, for the next couple of away matches at least!

Doctor's Orders

As well as food, I've always been partial to a drink. Now the health advice against over-indulgence is a relatively recent phenomenon, but even if it wasn't, our family doctor in Nuneaton was never a man who would tell you that a "wee drink" was bad for you!

Dr Kevin Flynn, our family GP, was club doctor at Nuneaton Borough. He and his lovely wife Betty lived in a fantastic big old five-bedroomed house on Lutterworth Road in Nuneaton. We often socialised with Kevin and Betty, and one night Kevin told me that the house was far too big for the two of them.

"I'm going to sell it, Noel. To you." I was shocked – CIP was doing well at and I had money in the bank, but I suppose I'd never considered myself worthy of a house on one of the town's premier thoroughfares.

"You're ready for this now, Noel." Kevin fixed me with a stare. He was right. We sold our bungalow and bought the house. Kevin and Betty moved to a smaller house just 150 yards down the road.

One winter's evening, we took Doctor and Mrs Flynn to a Sportsman's Evening at Coventry City Football Club. These lavish dinners with guest speakers took place once a month, and as a Vice President at

Coventry City these were a highlight for me. Every month for over twenty years I would take a table of ten and invite key clients and friends. On this particular occasion I had a very nasty cold, but there was no way I would miss the evening.

"Ah, you'll be fine, Noel – just wrap up warm and have a drop of Benylin" was Dr Flynn's advice. Fortunately there was a full bottle in the cabinet; I took a swig and popped it into my coat pocket.

The evening was great – it was easy to forget the blocked nose and cough while enjoying great entertainment. And I guess a couple or three whiskies helped. But when we came out into the cold at the end of the night, I felt rough again immediately. I glugged on the Benylin – swallowing half the bottle - and jumped into the car for the nine mile drive home.

Well, outside of alcohol I've never taken any form of recreational drug, but I can only imagine that my experience on the journey home was like some sort of trip. Three times I hallucinated that the road in front of me just disappeared to the left, and of course I steered to follow it! The third time this happened I bumped the kerb, twice, which was the first time my passengers noticed anything was awry – there were a couple of inches of snow on the roads, so they assumed I'd been slipping on the ice. I took my doctor's advice - "Slow down a bit, Noel!" - and we made it to his house.

"Leave the car here, come in for a drink," said Kevin. He was such a kind man that it was impossible to refuse. His hospitality was as Irish as can be – a huge whisky was thrust into my hand, with his usual advice, "don't ask for ice, it's bad for your stomach!

We chatted for quite a while – three whiskeys-worth of a while – before I decided it was time to head home. Joan and I managed the short walk no bother, but the biting cold (it was now 2.30am) had encouraged me to take another swig of Benylin – emptying the bottle - as we set off.

The rest is a blur. According to Joan, when we got into the house I took off my coat and jacket and said I was off to bed. The next thing Joan heard was a loud THUD! She ran from the kitchen to find me half way up the stairs, lying face down, unconscious, with a free-flowing waterfall of blood cascading from my nose down our cream stair carpet!

It would appear that I had put my hands into my trouser pockets before heading upstairs, and then either tripped or passed out. In an ideal, Benylin-free, world, I imagine the instinct to save myself would have made me pull my hands *out* of my pockets before thrusting them forwards. In this, I failed. And, perhaps my hands might have reached the stairs before my nose did. Again, I failed.

Instead, I appear to have pushed forward instinct-ively with my hands... while they were still in my pockets. So my suit trousers – my brand new suit trousers – were ripped to shreds. Having to replace the suit and the stair carpet was an expensive way to learn to take cough mixture in moderation!

LITTLE FECKER!

Florence Randle

Not all the good times were about food and alcohol. I always got immense pleasure from interacting with the fans – their enjoyment was what really made all the effort worthwhile.

Over the years I met many fans. Being Chairman, I suppose that as a rule, I was popular when the team did well, and not when times were hard. But one fan wasn't interested so in the results, as in the Chairman.

One Sunday lunchtime at the football club in the early 1980's, I was approached by a fan named Charles Randle and his son Andrew. They told me how Charles's grandma Florence was my biggest fan – she had cut photographs of me from press cuttings and put them on her wall. "Why has she done that?" I asked. "Because great-grandma thinks you're a very handsome man!" said little Andrew.

Charles explained that Florence was quite old, and in poor health - it would really cheer her up if she could meet me. Mother's Day was just a week away, so I said I would call round. I took Florence a bouquet of flowers, and though she was quite ill and tired, we had a cup of tea and a nice chat.

Sadly, Florence passed away a short time later. At a recent family event I had a drink with Charles and Andrew, and we recalled the lovely day when I met Florence. I was telling Charles about this book, and mentioned my first trip to see the Boro, the cup game against QPR in December 1953. "Yes, I was there too!" said Charles.

The Most Famous Men in the World

I end my account of the "good years" at Nuneaton Borough with my memories of two amazing men, both massive heroes of mine, who visited Manor Park during my tenure as Chairman. I set out to achieve something special at the club, both on and off the field. Looking back, even 30 years later, these two events were truly special.

George Best

George Best in a Nuneaton Borough shirt is a sight I'll never forget. He arrived with former Miss World Mary Stavin on his arm, and we had a late rush at the turnstiles as 4,317 poured into the ground. Besty only walked through the gates about half an hour before kick off and I think the message flew round the town that this wasn't a stunt, he was actually here!

On a cold March night, Coventry sent their first team and the match made the club about £7,000. To cap it all, Boro won 2-1, Best scored one goal and laid on the other. Whenever anyone talks about greedy football stars I always think of that match, when George Best gave something back to the game. It was a superb gesture - arranged by courtesy of Noel Cantwell. I still have the No. 7 Boro shirt worn that night by in my opinion the greatest player the world has ever seen.

I reproduce here, with his permission, a report on the occasion written by my good friend, Mike Malyon, after Best's tragic premature death in November 2005:

LITTLE FECKER!

A night to remember: Mike Malyon recalls how George Best weaved Manor Park magic as he led Nuneaton Borough against the Sky Blues...

GEORGE BEST promised Nuneaton Borough: 'I will not let you down.' But, more than that, he did them proud.

In one memorable night he showed why he will forever be ranked among the greatest.

After reaching the heights with Manchester United, after lifting the European Cup, after wowing them in the States, Best pulled on the shirt of non-league Nuneaton and was again hailed a superstar.

It was 1983 and Boro had a £40,000 tax bill. To raise money, the club made an audacious approach to Best, asking him to play at Manor Park in a friendly against First Division neighbours Coventry City. Many dismissed it as a pie-in-the-sky idea. Some scoffed at what was thought to be a publicity stunt.

Best, who was then going on 37, had officially retired from the professional game.

He had recently returned from playing in the American League and, in his own words, "was enjoying himself, going to the gym every day and playing in friendly matches up and down the country."

He was invited to take part in the Boro game by Noel Cantwell, who was a father figure during his days at Old Trafford.

Cantwell, who managed the Sky Blues in the late 60s, had been contacted by an old friend from Ireland, Boro director Sean Patterson.

The headline-grabbing announcement "Best to play for Nuneaton" was finalised during a lunchtime meeting at the Inn on the Park in London.

That was when Best said: "I will definitely be there. I am looking forward to it. I am playing well at the moment, so Coventry City had better look out."

A week later, on a bitter cold March night, in front of a 4,000-plus crowd, he was as good as his word.

Best arrived with a beauty queen on his arm, in the fur-coated shape of ex-Miss World Mary Stavin.

He looked fit and well. He signed autographs. He gave television interviews - and once on the pitch he conjured up 90 minutes of sheer class. The years rolled back and the skill shone through.

Coventry fielded their full first team, but all eyes were on Best. He was in midfield and began to show all the old touches, to give City's international full-back Danny Thomas a testing time

Bursts of acceleration may have been lacking - but Best was in fine form. He hit an inch-perfect 30-yard pass to lay on the opening goal after 23 minutes and eight minutes later Boro went 2-0 ahead - with a goal inspired and scored by Best.

A delicate pass with the outside of the foot found Paul Culpin. The striker slipped the ball to Richard

LITTLE FECKER!

Hill, who was hauled down by Melrose for a penalty.

Best stepped up, hardly pulled back his left foot but buried the spot kick past Les Sealey into the bottom corner.

City reduced the arrears just before half time through Dyson, who went back to his normal centre-half spot for the second half as Best drifted out wide but continued to dazzle.

Another superb pass saw Boro have a goal disallowed for offside. But they held on to their 2-1 lead. Then, at the final whistle, Best sprinted down the tunnel, as the fans swarmed on to the pitch to acclaim a brilliant individual performance.

The match raised a much-needed £7,000 for Boro - and at a reception in the town's George Eliot Hotel after the match, Best sipped a mineral water and announced he was considering offers of a playing comeback and a Hollywood film.

Neither actually happened. In the 20 years that followed, Best gradually lost his way.

Sadly, the footballer who was everyone's idol became his own worst enemy.

At the time of his Nuneaton appearance, Best was in one of his alcohol-free periods. And it showed.

He looked healthy and happy. But, a descent into a booze-fuelled lifestyle eventually left the once twinkled-toed, sparkling-eyed Irishman stumbling, dazed, ill and depressed.

This is not the way he should be remembered. Far better to recall his magic moments on the football field; the impish wizard in a scarlet red or emerald green shirt; that wondrous night at Wembley; those six FA Cup goals against Northampton; one marvellous volley at Highfield Road; the cheeky flicks; the balance-defying dribbles.

And, of course, that night in March 1983 when he became Nuneaton Borough's most famous signing, set Manor Park alight - and really was The Best.

Getting George Best, a personal and global hero, into Manor Park was an achievement that was going to be hard to surpass. I suppose a less ambitious man might have rested on his laurels. But just a year later, I had set my sights on an even more famous target, and I was pursuing another big – big – hero.

Muhammad Ali!

I'm a huge boxing fan. But you don't need to be to love Muhammad Ali. The man is a legend, one of most famous, most loved men in the world ever.

I was always on the lookout for publicity for the Boro. I heard that Ali was in Britain, touring boxing clubs, amazing grown-ups and inspiring the nation's youth. I pulled out all the stops, got hold of his schedule, found out he was coming to Birmingham. and negotiated and paid a fee.

My only thought was that the Boro fans deserved to have this unique man come through the gates.

LITTLE FECKER!

A proud moment

The date was set: Monday 7 May 1984. I spent two days chasing press and TV support for the event, but was gutted to find that the TV companies – BBC and ITV – had no camera crews or presenters available for the Monday because it was a bank holiday, and weren't able to pull resources together quickly enough to get the story in the press on the Friday. It did appear on the Saturday though!

Undaunted, I set everything up so that I would pick Ali up from his hotel in Birmingham and bring him to my home for a cup of tea before taking him to the match. I didn't arrange anything at the house, I simply wanted him to be there and meet Joan.

I was very excited in the lift up to his penthouse. Ali was sleek, not as heavy set as I expected him, as a heavyweight boxer, to be. He was handsome in a very smart blue suit – my first impression was of a male model. His personality was as impressive as his looks, the second I arrived his eyes and his arms opened wide and his face lit up in a huge smile.

There were a lot of people in the suite, family, friends, his entourage. He sat me down with a coffee and began to entertain me; magic tricks, stories, cheeky banter. The phone started ringing. Ali was busy, a couple of his friends motioned for me to pick the phone up. I did, but it kept ringing. I put it down and picked it up again – still it kept ringing.

"There must be another phone somewhere," I said. Then it stopped. Ali walked across the room towards me, a mischievous smile on his face, and he put a hand up close, behind my ear. The warbling phone noise was loud - he was making the sound himself, simply by rubbing his finger and thumb together.

We chatted and played around with magic for so long that there wasn't time to go to our house. I drove straight to Manor Park, with Ali following in the car behind with his chauffeur and assistant. We stopped near the ground and Ali and I transferred into the back of a bright yellow open-top 1920's Rolls Royce.

It was a bitterly cold Bank Holiday Monday, a morning kick off. The extreme weather was a factor, and barely 1,200 people turned out to welcome Ali. As the car pulled into the ground and onto the pitch the crowd erupted – I think once again no-one believed I could pull off such a coup – and they swarmed onto the pitch to follow the car.

LITTLE FECKER!

The chauffeur was as cool as the weather, I was worried the fans would damage his very special car, but smiling and relaxed, he edged the car around the ground. The crowd dispersed and Ali kicked footballs into the stands. He was clearly enjoying himself.

Ena Sharples! Get it?

Ali's appearance at Manor Park, for the Midland Floodlit Cup Final, Nuneaton Borough v Bedworth United, was his first, possibly his only, soccer match. We chatted throughout the game – at one point he asked me what the goal nets were for. Instead of giving a sensible answer, daft Ned said "Oh, we borrowed Ena Sharples's hair nets for the day." It was only after I'd said it that I realised the most famous man in the world had never heard of Ena Sharples.

Ali gave me one of his famous bug-eyed stares, as if I was talking nonsense, which I was. As I laughed to hide my embarrassment, a photographer captured the moment for posterity. The photo, above, now hangs in pubs in Dublin, Kilkenny, Malta and other places where I've had to send it to prove I wasn't making up the whole story!

Ali watched the whole game, a draw, and presented the shared trophy to the two captains. Then he entertained us in the boardroom with more magic tricks, while posing for photographs with all comers.

I'm not sure who did the catering that day – I would normally have taken charge of it myself, but I was busy making sure our guest made it to Manor Park. In the boardroom I watched Muhammad Ali – a devout Muslim - pick up a soggy-looking sandwich.

As he was about to bite into it, one of his minders said, "That's pig, brother. You mustn't eat it." Ali lifted the sandwich to eye level, then calmly removed the *ham* and put it in an ashtray. There were a few red faces around!

When it was time for him to leave, Ali gave me a huge hug and thanked me for a fascinating day!

Despite a disappointing attendance, it was a golden memory. First Best, then Ali. How could I top that?

I met Ali again twenty-five years later, when he returned to Britain in 2009, ravaged by Parkinsons Disease. Clearly very ill, he still showed flashes of his former self, his wicked humour and appetite for mischief. I gave him a copy of the photo of the two of us; he nodded and smiled and passed to his wife, who looked at it and thanked me with a tear in her eye.

Did I say I knew how to pick my fights?

Half Time: Analysis

I was Nuneaton Borough Chairman for ten problem-filled, costly, but exhilarating years. Golden years, never-to-be-forgotten memories. Days I'd never trade.

We achieved so much: founder members and twice runners up of the Alliance Premier League; 13 players graduating into Football League; 7 First Round FA Cup appearances; 3 FA Trophy quarter finals. Several Midland Floodlit and Birmingham Senior Cup wins; invited 3 times to the Anglo-Italian tournament. We purchased and improved our ground, and welcomed George Best and Muhammad Ali as our guests.

Yet overnight, everything we achieved was forgotten. "New brooms" appeared. They didn't sweep clean, but they swept all aside.

The "second half" of my story, **Dirty Feckers**, is dominated by events at Nuneaton Borough Football Club, and in the High Courts of Justice. It tells of how I - a *Little Fecker* from the outskirts of Dublin - was stripped to the bone by a conspiracy of greedy individuals, aided and abetted by a corrupt system.

And it shows how guts, determination and humour - present in everything Irish - maintained me through the darkest of days, to emerge - grinning, singing, *triumphant*.

The story isn't quite complete. But it will be, soon. And then I'll publish what happened next.

Personal Postscript

As you've read, my life hasn't been easy. I've had to fight battles with my wits, and sometimes with my fists. When I could see the enemy, I won many more fights than I lost. And if I did lose, I smiled and got up to fight another day.

I always fancied my chances in a fair fight. But the enemy I was about to face wasn't prepared to face me. And certainly wasn't prepared to fight fair.

I've come a long way, in every sense, from the fields of County Dublin. With little going for me other than a lot of energy and a little bit of charm, I've reached some heady heights.

I trained with Barry McGuigan, and sat with George Best and Muhammad Ali. How was I going to top that? Truth is, I didn't think I could. But I didn't need to. I was happy.

I often think of Mammy and Daddy, and hope they'd be proud of Ned, their cheeky seventh child. I think about my pals in Ireland, and imagine they'd reckon the *Little Fecker* has done all right.

I sincerely hope that you've enjoyed my journey so far, and I thank you for your interest.

I look forward to seeing you for the second half.

Noel Kelly, March 2014

I was on top of the world. But for some, the top of the world was not Noel Kelly's rightful place. I was an uneducated, happy-go-lucky Paddy, and educated, well-to-do local folk were getting jealous.

Nothing I learned on my way up, on my way out of the field and into the boardroom, could have prepared me for what came next.

Find out what happened to Noel Kelly next, in

Dirty Feckers

The Fall of Noel Kelly

Coming soon!

Made in the USA
Charleston, SC
12 March 2014